Basics About Disabilities
and Science and Engineering Education

Basics About Disabilities and Science and Engineering Education

February, 2011

Ruta Sevo, Ph.D., Researcher and Writer

Under direction of Robert L. Todd, Principal Investigator

Center for Assistive Technology and Environmental Access
(CATEA)
Georgia Institute of Technology
http://www.catea.gatech.edu

© Copyright 2011 Ruta Sevo. The report may be copied and printed for non-commercial distribution.

Print ISBN 978-0-9831588-8-2

The report is available free as a PDF from http://stores.lulu.com/sevo. Print and other electronic versions (Kindle, EPUB) are available at cost. It is an ad hoc report, not a publication of the National Science Foundation or the Georgia institute of Technology.

 The material is based upon work supported by the National Science Foundation under Grant HRD 0622885. Any opinions, findings, and conclusions or recommendations expressed are those of the authors and do not necessarily reflect the views of the National Science Foundation or the Georgia Institute of Technology.

Cover photo: Sprinter's carbon leg invented by Van Phillips, 1990s

Citation: Sevo, Ruta (2011). *Basics about disabilities and science and engineering education.* Atlanta, GA. Under the direction of Robert L. Todd, Center for Assistive Technology and Environmental Access, Georgia Institute of Technology,.

Abstract: An introduction to disability issues, history, laws, and research for educators who have little or no experience with students or colleagues with disabilities. There is a short overview in the form of a presentation script. A section looks at the need for inclusion and recruitment of students with disabilities to science and engineering fields, and gives examples of resources for faculty to improve instruction. The Short Reader and Syllabus is a digest covering topics often included in full Disability Studies readers written by experts. An annotated bibliography is provided for those who want further depth. It draws from syllabi used for undergraduates.

The Center for Assistive Technology and Environmental Access (CATEA), Georgia Institute of Technology is a multidisciplinary engineering and design research center dedicated to enhancing the health, activity and participation of people with functional limitations through the application of assistive and universally designed technologies in real world environments, products and devices. See http://www.catea.gatech.edu/

TABLE OF CONTENTS

INTRODUCTION — 1
What is the purpose of this resource? How is it organized and how can you use it?

SHORT OVERVIEW — 5
An overview in the form of a slide presentation with a script

SCIENCE AND ENGINEERING EDUCATION AND THE PARTICIPATION OF PERSONS WITH DISABILITIES — 41
How many people with disabilities are in science and engineering fields now? Why do we want more to join? What kind of support is available for students and faculty to encourage participation?

A SHORT READER AND SYLLABUS FOR DISABILITY STUDIES — 65
A survey of topics like basic statistics, history, research, and standards. A digest of material you typically find in Disability Studies readers written by experts.

CHANGING OUR PSYCHOLOGICAL RESPONSE — 171
Is it possible to change a response to disabilities and counter traditional and conditioned thoughts and feelings?

APPENDIX A: A LIST OF LAWS   181

              What kinds of issues turned into legal mandates? A
              chronology.

APPENDIX B: TOP RECOMMENDED RESOURCES   191

              First-resort sources if you want to learn more.

APPENDIX C: ANNOTATED BIBLIOGRAPHY   195

              Annotated citations in support of the Short Reader
              above, for a more comprehensive follow-up.

ACKNOWLEDGEMENTS   211

INTRODUCTION

This book is for educators who have not thought about disabilities and who have little or no experience with students or colleagues with disabilities. The goal is to introduce the topic and give the reader a handle on basics and context.

Sections are designed for different depth and interests.

The **Short Overview** is self-explanatory. A starting point.

The section called **Science and Engineering Education and the Participation of Persons With Disabilities** looks at the need for inclusion. Why do we need to tap students with disabilities for study in science and engineering? What are we doing to recruit and support them?

The **Short Reader and Syllabus** is a digest for those who want more but probably not as much as a full reader in Disability Studies with chapters written by experts. Here, whole articles are summarized in one page. The articles are mostly selected from ones commonly read in beginning courses in Disability Studies. The Short Reader covers the history of our treatment of people with disabilities, for example, and the disability rights movement. It gives you examples of social science research on discrimination and the sociology of people with disabilities. Hopefully, the Reader helps explain our complex social and psychological encounter with disability.

Changing Our Psychological Response is for educators who might want to know that we can learn to moderate any automatic, unconscious biases when we interact with people with disabilities.

Finally, the **Annotated Bibliography** is for someone who wants to find the sources.

ASSUMPTIONS

Everyone needs to know more about disabilities. Any one of us is or can become a person with a disability overnight. There are profound dynamics in play when able-bodied people interact with people with disabilities. Historically, Western society has gone the gamut in treatment from charity, to murder, to freak shows, to empathy, and respect.

We will assume that we as a society want to evolve to a point where the response to a disability is not inhumanity and injustice. We will assume that the reader agrees that a person with a disability should not be excluded from community, public life, and work. It has taken much of the 20th Century to reach a point in America where children with disabilities are included in public schools and many people with disabilities live in the community, appear in public, and work, including as professionals and leaders.

At a minimum, we can appreciate that the negative treatment of persons with disabilities is grounded in social and historical constructs, or traditions, that are obsolete and destructive.

Since any one of us is or can become a member of the group, **our motivation to learn can start with self-awareness and self-interest**.

WHY THIS PRODUCT?

Much has changed fairly recently: the disability rights movement, new laws, the field of Disability Studies, the rise of comprehensive special education services, and the availability of new assistive technologies. Many adults in our working population are not familiar with them.

People working in education, workforce development, or diversity programs have little time to keep up with related fields. Professionals in science and engineering may not have time to read social science literature, whether on diversity issues, discrimination, or disabilities. Yet we all encounter persons with disabilities in our public life and in our workplace. In our work life, we may be in the position of interviewing or being interviewed by, hiring and developing persons with disabilities. Or, we have a disability, and we want to understand our situation better.

There are many other good sources for Disability Studies, from rich web sites (both academic and communally written) to published works written by experts. Some are listed in a section at the end. None is composed covering this range of topics.

BARRIERS TO INTEREST: UNCONSCIOUS REACTIONS

Is there a reluctance to engage this topic? Accounts from history, psychology, and sociology tell us that society struggles with the idea of disability and with persons with disabilities. There are old beliefs that a disability is God's punishment, a mark of moral turpitude, a contamination of the human race, a genetic failure. These beliefs alienate us from the topic. Disability is stigmatized – it has been viewed as a condition to be shunned and avoided. It has been considered unlucky, painful, limiting – a dark side of life around us. We fear contamination or inconvenience and are reluctant to be reminded of our own vulnerabilities. People with disabilities average among the most economically disadvantaged groups in society. In short, it is unpleasant to think about it, if we are able-bodied.

If we are disabled, it means we may struggle for dignity, respect, and independence, and might be assisted by appliances and people. We may feel anger about poor treatment, negative attitudes and expectations, paternalism served along with the help, discrimination, and lack of access to activities including work that we know is possible for us with or without the right help.

Many in the disability community say that the biggest barriers to their independence and dignity are negative expectations and misinformation.

One of the biggest barriers might be mutual frustration. We don't have much experience with a world in which our buildings, sidewalks-cars-buses-planes, computer interfaces, communication devices (phones, ATMs, public announcement systems), and public services *anticipate a truly wide variety in abilities among us.* A world in which jobs are flexible and allow more people to work. We are going to hit the hard edges for some time. One thing we can do is learn more about the goal.

BARRIERS TO UNDERSTANDING: COLLIDING SOCIAL CONSTRUCTS

Definitions of "disability" have shifted over time, of course. But they differ in recent time, fundamentally, because of changes in mental models about disability. An outsider cannot learn this easily. Insiders might take offense at words or concepts of disability that are outdated, unsophisticated, or implicitly insulting, in their view.

For example, the "social model" is the view that our social and architectural environments "create disability," and that many people with disabilities could participate if not for traditional barriers. The disability rights movement expressed this view in campaigning for legal rights to integrate into society, to live independently, to receive new kinds of services, and to expect legally-required architectural and design modifications. The "medical model" is older, and focuses on the individual and the "broken body," and alternatives for cure, rehabilitation, and adaptation to typical living environments. (These models are described further in the Reader section.)

One theory did not replace the other; they are active in parallel in our public discourse. Policies and laws are based in one or the other, posing inconsistencies of interpretation and application. For example, the policies underlying Social Security services are premised in the medical model, and the Americans With Disabilities Act is premised in the social model. It takes some analysis to understand the thinking behind the way certain services and programs classify and treat children and persons with disabilities: identifying students eligible for special education, counting population via the U.S. census, accepting trainees into rehabilitation and training programs, qualifying people for Federal assistance. National and international standards can be inconsistent with each other as they evolve.

Consequently, an attempt to describe the world of disability is difficult and contentious. Older sources will use older (and now offending) words. The medical diagnosis of diseases and disorders is fluid, for example, the criteria used to determine that someone has a learning disability such as ADHD changes. Statistical measures related to disability can vary depending on definitions and classifications. Even authoritative measures of disability or population (e.g., "rate of employment") can yield confusing numbers. As one source puts it, the category of "disabled" is unstable.[1]

---

[1] Further explored in depth in Barnartt, Sharon (2010). *Disability as a fluid state*. Research in Social Science and Disability. Emerald Group Publishing. Recommended by advisor Corinne Kirchner.

SHORT OVERVIEW

slide 0:	Titles
slide 1:	Anyone Can Join
slide 2:	Why Talk About it?
slide 3:	Keeping Up with Change
slide 4:	Invisible and Visible
slide 5:	How Many?
slide 6:	What About Science and Engineering?
slide 7:	Trends in the Educational Pipeline
slide 8:	Undergraduate Students
slide 9:	Support to Faculty
slide 10:	CAST
slide 11:	AHEAD
slide 12:	SciTrain Project
slide 13:	Learning Disabilities
slide 14:	Civil Rights Movement Compared with Disability Rights Movement
slide 15:	Big Change After the 1970's
slide 16:	Hot Spots in Bioethics
slide 17:	Teaching Tolerance
slide 18:	Historical Themes
slide 19:	Twentieth Century (Pre Disability Rights Movement)
slide 20:	Universal Design
slide 21:	People-First Language
slide 22:	Stigma

slide 23:   Story of Prosthetics
slide 24:   Why Do We Need to Tap this Pool of Students?
slide 25:   The Ultimate Goal
slide 26:   Center for Assistive Technology and Environmental Access, Georgia Tech

SLIDE 0:

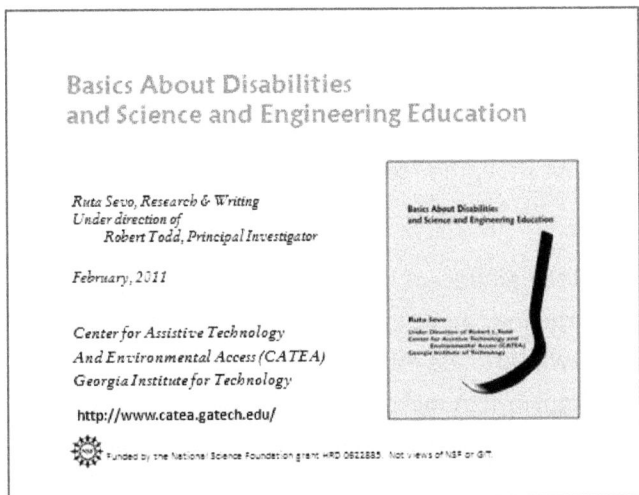

SLIDE 1:

Robert Murphy was an anthropologist at Columbia University who acquired paraplegia at age 52 due to a tumor on his spinal cord. He published an ethnography about his experience, called *The Body Silent*, acting as a "participant observer." (His study was funded by the National Science Foundation.)

"There is a clear pattern ... of prejudice towards the disabled and debasement of their social status. This is manifested in its most extreme forms by avoidance, fear, and outright hostility. ... The disabled occupy the same devalued status as ex-convicts, certain ethnic and racial minorities, and the mentally ill. ... The physically impaired person ... is given a negative identity by society, and much of his social life is a struggle against this imposed image. ... The greatest impediment to a person's taking full part in his society is not his physical flaws, but rather the tissue of myths, fears, and misunderstandings that society attaches to them."

He says that disability subverts the American ideal of the youthful, clean and lean body. He uses the words dehumanization, the "contaminated outsider," the "quasi-human," and "alien species."

People recoil from visible reminders of imperfection and reminders of their own vulnerability. Social interaction can be tense and forced, as each party struggles with ambiguity. The mutual awkwardness must be suppressed and disavowed. The able-bodied must pretend that the impairment makes no difference. The impaired person must become an expert at putting others at ease.

Murphy and a friend with a disability organized a program at a library to explain their experience. They expected a large crowd. Few came. He realized that his former friends and neighbors were "repelled by the subject," and were now ambivalent toward him. "The old social me had died," he wrote.

SLIDE 2:

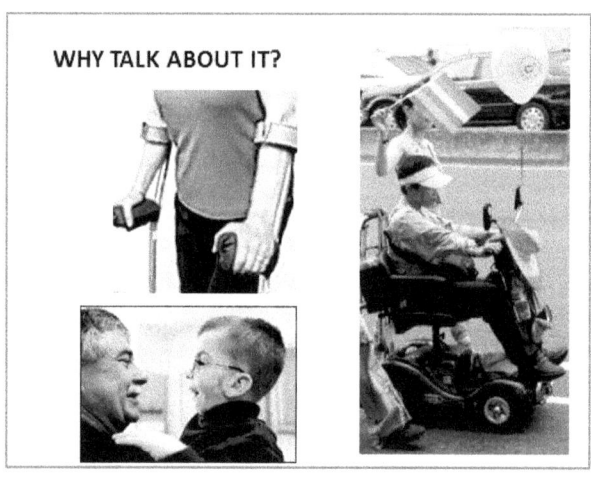

This is a topic that is hard to engage. We notice differences among people and develop in-group preferences before the age of one. We decipher meaning associated with differences, with or without the help of adults, forming assumptions and stereotypes that are convenient ways to organize our social world. As Robert Murphy observed, impairments are a form of difference categorized as undesirable, deviant, and "other."

History, psychology, religion, and sociology tell us that society struggles with the idea that some people will be disabled. We have seen impairment as the work of the devil, as God's punishment, as a mark of moral turpitude, a contamination of the human race, or as a genetic failure. These beliefs alienate us from the topic. The topic itself is stigmatized. It is the "dark side" of life—misfortune. We fear contamination or inconvenience. If you are able-bodied, it is unpleasant to think about it.

The biggest barriers to the independence, dignity and respect of persons with disabilities are the negative responses and misinformation among people around them.

The biggest barriers to **changing** our negative responses and misinformation are **psychological**—understanding and tolerating impairments, and **cognitive**—knowing enough to reduce our fear, reluctance, and awkwardness.

The aim of this introduction is to **reduce misinformation**, and to **encourage reflection** on our own responses.

SLIDE 3:

> **KEEPING UP WITH CHANGE**
>
> Hard for "outsiders" to grasp all that's happened:
>
> - Disability Rights Movement
> - Laws on rights to jobs, special education, accommodation
> - Assistive technologies
> - Support services in colleges
> - Field of Disability Studies
> - The "medical model" versus the "social model" of disability in society

Another barrier is the rapid change in how we think about disability. It is hard for "outsiders" to keep up with changes—greater sophistication in our understanding, and words we use.

A revolution in our treatment of people with disabilities occurred with the Disability Rights movement that took momentum in the 1960s and following. New laws against discrimination and for inclusive, special education have changed conditions dramatically. Disability Studies is now an established academic field. Assistive technologies are making it possible for students to learn and enter the workforce in spite of disability. Colleges have made accommodations and offer support services.

There are inconsistencies in our thinking, in the way various government programs and laws define "disability," in how we define and measure "disability."

An older view is called the "medical model." It focuses on a disability as a medical problem, and "the broken body." The focus is on curing or fixing the impairment, offering rehabilitation, and hoping that the individual can adapt to typical living environments.

A newer view is called the "social model." It is the view that our social and architectural environments "create disability." Many people with impairments can function very well and participate fully, if not for traditional barriers. We need to change society's view of disability as a deficiency, and treat disability as a consequence of environments. We need to make our physical environments and educational practices more flexible, to allow for a greater variety in abilities.

SLIDE 4:

One of the most famous disabled scientists is the physicist Stephen Hawking, who has had Lou Gehrig's disease for more than 26 years. He can no longer speak and can barely move. He is still a professor at Cambridge University. He is an example of a professional who became disabled after he established a professional reputation.

A number of notable scientists have been retrospectively diagnosed for possible intellectual disabilities. Albert Einstein might have had dyslexia—he had a bad memory for simple things like months of the year. He may never have learned to tie his shoelaces. He may have had Asperger's also—he could not speak well until the age of nine. His parents thought he was retarded. He attended a ceremony without socks (a common irritation to those with Asperger's).

Leonardo Da Vinci had dyslexia—he wrote his notes backwards. Alfred Nobel had epileptic seizures.

Michaelangelo possibly had Obsessive Compulsive Disorder—he had a short temper, avoided people, walked out on conversations, slept in his clothes, and worked in isolation for long periods of time. Darwin stuttered and possibly had OCD.

There are inventors who were driven to solve a problem posed by their own impairment. Louis Braille, who became blind after he accidentally stabbed himself in the eye with his father's awl, invented Braille (the embossed symbols that enable tactile reading by blind people). Alexander Graham Bell invented the telephone to help his deaf mother.

SLIDE 5:

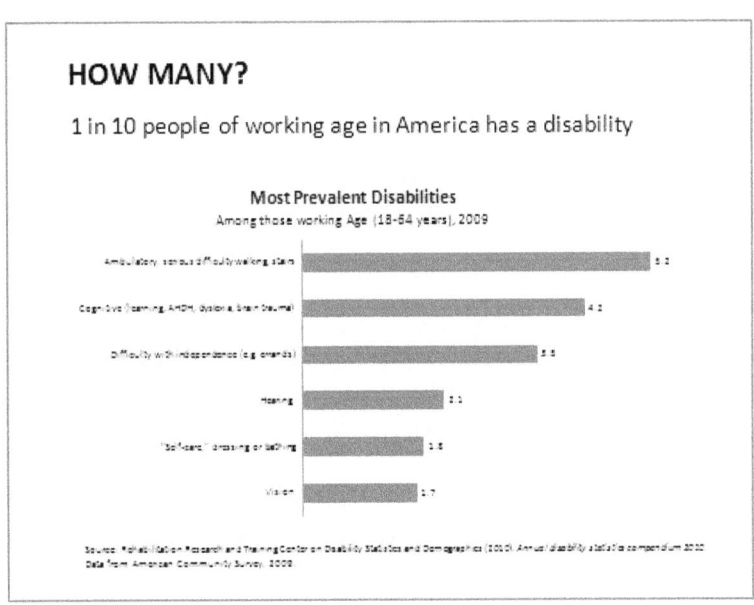

One in ten people of working age in America has a disability. (The Census Bureau says "1 in 5" but that is counting the whole population, which includes those over 65.)

Most Prevalent Disabilities, Working Age (18-64 years), 2009

Vision	1.7
"Self-care," dressing or bathing	1.8
Hearing	2.1
Difficulty with independence (e.g. errands)	3.5
Cognitive (learning, AHDH, dyslexia, brain trauma)	4.2
Ambulatory, serious difficulty walking, stairs	5.2

Source: Rehabilitation Research and Training Center on Disability Statistics and Demographics (2010). Annual disability statistics compendium 2010.

Among adults of working age, the most prevalent disability is "difficulty walking or using stairs" (5.2%), followed by a cognitive disability (4.2%), hearing disability (2.1%). About 1.8% have difficulty dressing or bathing, and 3.5% have difficulty running errands.

It is estimated that roughly 15% of persons with disabilities were *born* with their disability. 85% were disabled *after birth*, due to illness, accidents, war and other causes.

About 35% of persons with disabilities of working age are employed. This is less than half the rate of employment for able-bodied people (74%).

SLIDE 6:

WHAT ABOUT SCIENCE AND ENGINEERING?

- About 11% of undergraduates in S&E fields
- More than half have learning disabilities
- 1% of people holding Ph.D.'s in S&E
- The number of full-time faculty with disabilities in S&E is about 10,300
- In faculty positions, 20,000 persons with disabilities (2006)
- Percentage of annual doctorates awarded is about 1.7%

Committee on Equal Opportunities in Science and Engineering (2009). Broadening participation in America's STEM workforce 2007-2008

About **11 percent of undergraduate** students in science and engineering fields have one or more disabilities and the percentage tracks with the frequency in the general population of 15-24 year olds.

More than **half (of that 11 percent of students with disabilities) have LEARNING disabilities**.

Only **1 percent of people holding Ph.D.'s** in science and engineering report having disabilities.

The number of **full-time faculty** in science and engineering fields with disabilities is **about 10,300**.

There were over **20,000** persons with disabilities **in faculty positions** in science and engineering fields in 2006.

The percentage of annual **doctorates awarded** to persons with disabilities is about **1.7%**.

More people with disabilities are coming up the ranks than before.

SLIDE 7:

> TRENDS IN THE EDUCATIONAL PIPELINE
>
> - We prevent more disabilities (w/medical interventions, reduced rate of accidents)
> - We identify more mental illness
> - We educate more through special education
> - Persons with disabilities are more visible in community
> - Rising:
>   - Autism
>   - ADHD
>   - Depression

Our ability to prevent certain disabilities is much improved, for example, avoiding medical complications that lead to blindness, deafness, brain damage; the care of premature babies; standards and practices that reduce accidents and injuries (e.g., motorcycle and bicycle helmets).

New learning disabilities have been identified. They include Attention Deficit Disorder with Hyperactivity (ADHD) in 1980, and Post Traumatic Stress Disorder. The definitions of **depression** have expanded. It is **now the single most common psychiatric disorder**, accounting for more than one quarter of all patient visits. **About half of psychiatric patients receive prescriptions.** Prozac, valium and other drugs have become very common.

All U.S. public schools are required to offer a free and appropriate education to children with disabilities. **In 2008, about 13% of public school enrollment received special education. The largest group within that 13% (39%) have learning disabilities.** The second largest group (22%) has speech or language impairments.

Learning disabilities as a category was introduced in 1963. Now it is **the largest category of children served**.

The expansion and sophistication of special education, located in mainstream schools, has made **persons with disabilities more visible.** This helps change attitudes, understanding, and experience. **People are more aware of the potential for treatment and interventions among various childhood mental impairments**.

The numbers of children diagnosed as autistic or ADHD is rising dramatically. The causes are not known. It is estimated that **3%-7% of school-aged children have ADHD and 1% have a variation of autism**.

With the recognition of **Post Traumatic Stress Syndrome (PTSD),** we have many more veterans needing and expecting care, and new specializations in research and care of PTSD.

The scope of **widening diagnoses of mental illness** has resulted in greater numbers of people identified as mentally ill, and medicated. The cause of many conditions is not known.

SLIDE 8:

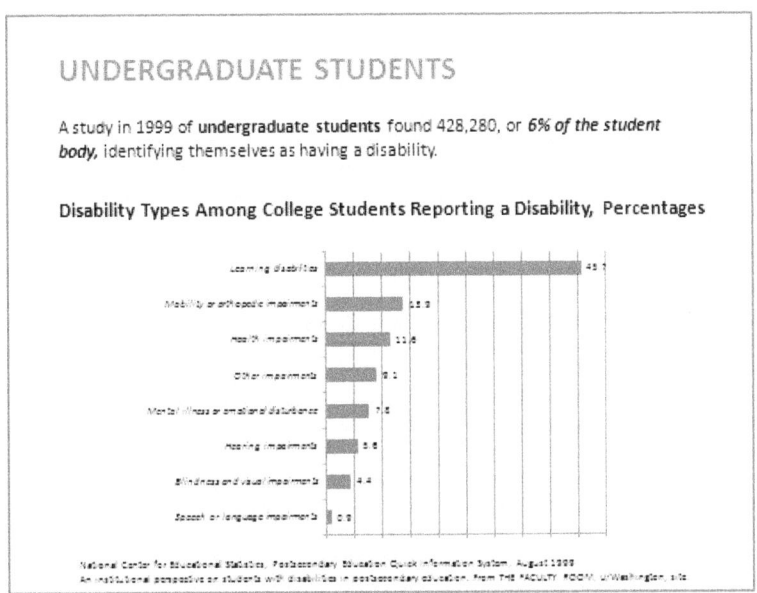

About **11 percent of undergraduate** students in science and engineering fields have one or more impairments and the percentage tracks with the frequency in the general population of 15-24 year olds. (Per 2009 report by Committee on Equal Opportunities in Science and Engineering, 2009)

More than **half have learning disabilities**. (That is **5-6% of college students in STEM**.)

A number of laws require reasonable accommodation in education and in the workplace.

- Education for All Handicapped Children Act of 1975
- Individuals with Disabilities Education Act of 2004 (IDEA)
- Americans with Disabilities Act of 1990 (ADA)
- Assistive Technology Act of 1998 (AT Act)

The field of assistive technologies has grown tremendously in the last decades. It includes the development of **prosthetics** (artificial body parts), **implants** (in the ear, hear, pumps for diabetics), **alternative communications tools** (visual alternatives to sound for deaf people, Braille and sound for blind people, software to organize and check text for dyslexics, alternative input devices using voice/mouth/breath/eye signals).

A number of organizations help faculty as they seek to assimilate and incorporate ways to make higher education more accessible. They typically provide guides organized by particular disabilities, case studies, videos of students with disability describing what helps them function better.

They are implementing principles called **Universal Design for Instruction, developed starting only in 1998.**

Universal Design of Instruction or Universal Design for Learning address the design of instruction in school settings so that it is accessible to students with learning and other disabilities. It includes, for example, using multiple ways to deliver information (lectures, learning groups, hands-on experience, and field work) and sensitivity to the physical environment of the classroom.

SLIDE 9:

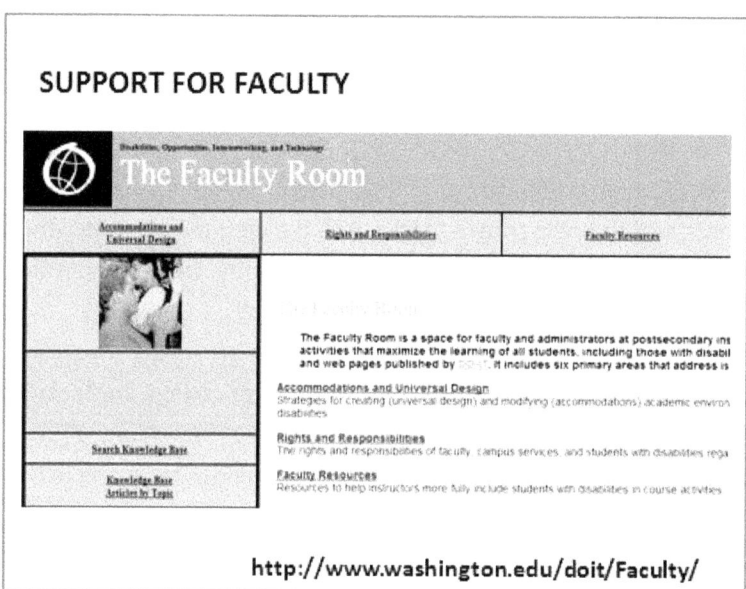

One example of support for implementing Universal Design of Instruction is the **FACULTY ROOM** on the University of Washington website, within the Project DO-IT website. It explains **what is available** as an assist, listed by various impairments. There are links to **case studies**, associations for students having the impairment, and typical supports. There are videos of **students explaining what is helpful** to them.

The website explains **how to anticipate accommodations** in all the typical learning environments – what to do differently, if you have a student with an impairment, or, want to **anticipate preferences** and needs from different brains:

- Large Lectures
- Group work
- Test Taking
- Field Work
- Science Labs
- Computer Labs
- Adaptive Technology
- Web Pages
- Distance Learning
- Artwork
- Writing Assignments
- International/Travel Programs

SLIDE 10:

An organization called CAST runs the National Center on Universal Design for Learning as of 2009, providing curriculum examples to teachers at all levels, as well as technical assistance, online and in-person courses, and resource materials.

SLIDE 11:

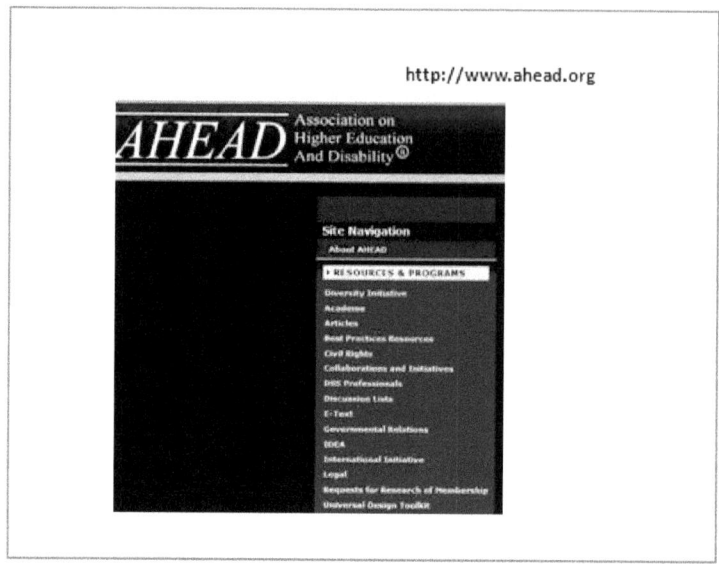

The Association on Higher Education and Disability (AHEAD) offers standards for disability programs.

SLIDE 12:

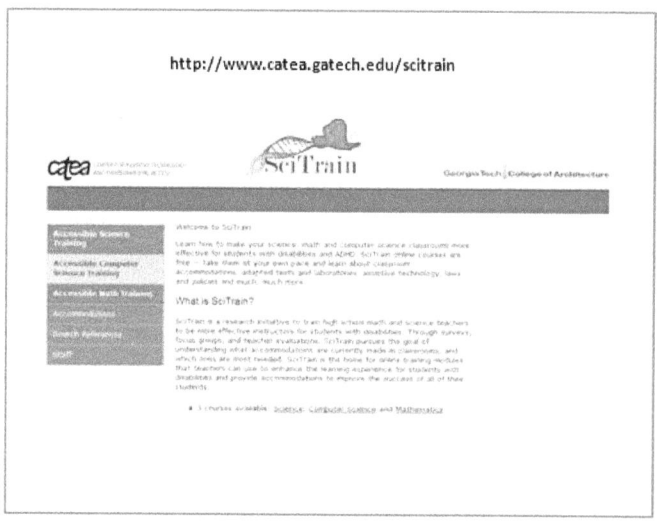

There are projects that are researching **how best to teach mathematics, science, and computer science** to students with disabilities.

The project SciTrain at Georgia Tech is finding out what effective instructors are doing now, for students with disabilities, and what kinds of things they could do to be more effective.

It offers **online training modules** that teachers can use in these courses.

SciTrain U offers tools for faculty and courses in higher education. There is a tutorial called **"Accessible STEM Teaching 101"** to answer many of the questions that instructors have who have never before taught a student with a disability. The site also offers a guide called **"Improved Teaching for Large Lecture Classes"** that summarizes things that an instructor in any subject can do, to accommodate a wider range of students.

The project is housed in the Center for Assistive Technology and Environmental Access, and is led by Robert L. Todd, who sponsored this product with funding from the National Science Foundation.

SLIDE 13:

LEARNING DISABILITIES

- DEVELOPMENTAL or COGNITIVE disability
  from birth
  Intellectual disability ("mental retardation") IQ <70
  Down syndrome
  Autism (1% of children)
  Aspergers
  Attention-Deficit-Hyperactivity Disorder (3-7% of children)

- MENTAL ILLNESS :
  Post Traumatic Stress
  Bipolar
  Depression (50% of psychiatric care)
  Schizophrenia

Learning disabilities are an "invisible" impairment. The majority of students in special education (39%) have learning disabilities.

Learning disabilities are **developmental and cognitive disorders**—the brain processes information differently. **They are usually present from birth. One form is** a **severe limitation in intelligence**—an IQ of 70/75. However, some people with learning disabilities, for example, autism, have a very high IQ.

Autism, Asperger's, and Attention-Deficit Hyperactivity Disorder are learning disabilities. A child has difficulty interacting socially, or has abnormal levels of inattention and/or hyperactivity. There are **no know cures** but early intervention can improve functioning and management of behaviors.

These are both separate from **mental illness**. Learning disabilities and mental retardation are evident from birth or appear early in childhood. Mental illness can be caused by disease, trauma, and genes. It does not imply low intelligence or learning difficulties. For example, **Post Traumatic Stress** can occur as a result of a traumatic event. **Bipolar disorder, depression**, and **schizophrenia** are examples. Mental illness is **treatable** and **can be cured or managed** through medication or psychosocial treatment.

- About 13% of children have a developmental disability , including autism
- About 1% of children in the US have Autism Spectrum Disorder
- Autism is 4-5 time more likely to occur in boys than in girls
- About 40% of children with an ASD do not talk at all
- ASD appears by age 2 (80% of the time)
- 3-7% of children in school have ADHD
- The prevalence of ADHD increased an average of 3% per year from 1997 to 2006
- Prevalence varies between states (5% to 11%)
- Workers with ADHD are more likely to have at least one sick day in the past month
- About 1.2% to 1.6% of children have intellectual disability (a.k.a. mental retardation)

SLIDE 14:

All the rights movements sought laws to **ban discrimination** and grant **equal rights** to housing, education, employment, and other public services.

Persons with disabilities **need**, besides a ban on discrimination, **access to medical and rehabilitation services**. They need **choice in medical treatment**. They need **structural modifications in public spaces** and transport. They need **reasonable accommodation from employers**. They need c**ommunity-based support services** in order to live independently.

Most critically, our ordinary physical environments embed a bias against a certain range of ability (sight, hearing, mobility, agility). The design of our living spaces and tools, public and private, assume a range of ability that creates disability. There is great inertia in changing physical design of products and architectural structures.

"If you remove discrimination against women and minorities (and others), they flourish and participate. With disabled people, **you have both discrimination and real limitations**. If all social barriers are removed, the impaired person does not become equally enabled." Resources are needed to change both social and physical barriers. The government plays a large role in providing services and regulating access to the services.

Also, people with **invisible disabilities** are often reluctant to self-identify, or identify with the movement, to avoid stigma and stereotyping.

Further, unlike gender or race, **the attribute of "disability" or "impairment" is not clear-cut**. A wide range of impairments are lumped together in the phrase "persons with disabilities." Each individual encounters unique circumstances, in terms of the implication for functioning in society. Our approach to special education has recognized that "one size does not fit all" for children with impairments, and each requires his or her own plan based on needs. There are degrees of "difference," stigma, and challenge. The individual's experience, and society response to that individual, is not as predictable as it might be based on gender or skin color.

The attribute of race has also become "unstable," in census taking and statistics, for example. People are rejecting simplistic categories and labels, especially when they carry negative social connotations.

SLIDE 15:

BIG CHANGES AFTER THE 1970s

BEFORE
- Residence in institutions isolated from the community
- Patronization by caretakers ("the helping industry")
- Many physical barriers to mobility in public places
- No accommodation for deafness or blindness in public areas
- Limited employment options
- Exclusion from public presence
- No persons with disabilities teaching or running institutions for the disabled
- Small advocacy organizations for a few subgroups (blind, deaf, some diseases)

AFTER
- National advocacy organizations; self-advocacy; strong parent groups
- Removal of physical barriers in public places, by law
- Public transportation designed for assistance
- Ban on employment discrimination, by law
- Signage and interfaces for the hard of hearing and visually impaired
- Entrance into professional positions in general
- Jobs as teachers and administrators serving the disabled open up
- Assistive technologies research and products flourish
- Rise of independent living centers and support networks
- Biographical and anthropological testimonials to experience and discrimination
- Rise of Disability Studies
- Rise of special education in schools, integrated into mainstream
- National identity for persons with disabilities as a group and as a movement

During a few decades starting in the early 1970s, **a great transformation occurred** in the lives of people with disabilities in the U.S. We can characterize the change as follows:

BEFORE
- Residence in institutions isolated from the community
- Patronization by caretakers ("the helping industry")
- Many physical barriers to mobility in public places
- No accommodation for deafness or blindness in public areas
- Limited employment options

- Exclusion from public presence
- No persons with disabilities teaching or running institutions for disabled people
- Small advocacy organizations for a few subgroups (blind, deaf, some diseases)

AFTER
- National advocacy organizations; self-advocacy; strong parent groups
- Removal of physical barriers in public places, by law
- Public transportation designed for assistance
- Ban on employment discrimination, by law
- Signage and interfaces for the hard of hearing and visually impaired
- Entrance into professional positions in general
- Jobs as teachers and administrators serving disabled people open up
- Assistive technologies research and products flourish
- Rise of independent living centers and support networks
- Biographical and anthropological testimonials to experience and discrimination
- Rise of Disability Studies
- Rise of special education in schools, integrated into mainstream
- National identity for persons with disabilities as a group and as a movement

SLIDE 16:

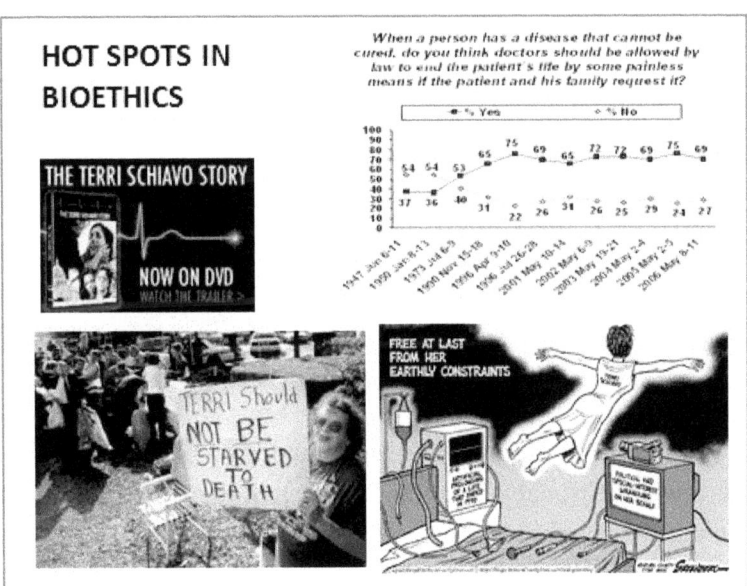

Big questions in bioethics that arise related to disabilities are: the right to be born, the right to die, and the right to treatment. The answers are deeply felt and rarely clear-cut.

Historically, persons with disabilities have been treated less-than-human, and devalued. There is a greater impact for people with impairments such as mental retardation (now among "developmental disabilities") or severe disfigurement. Fundamentally, the issues are rooted in judgments about the sanctity of life and the quality of life.

The disability rights movement protested the dominance of medical professionals over life decisions and raised awareness of patient rights, and the need for consumer/patient protection from biased and misinformed decisions.

Newborns with impairments. Should an infant born with Down syndrome, spina bifida, a severe bowel obstruction, or breathing problems, be treated for related problems, when the chances for survival are low, and the quality of life after treatment is extremely limited? Treatment has been denied, even with concurrence from parents.

Prenatal testing and selective abortion. If prenatal testing shows the presence of certain impairments that are assumed to indicate significant suffering and limited quality of life, is it justified to abort? Disability rights advocates maintain that selective abortion is biased, misused, and based on misinformation about quality of life.

Sustaining life with a disability. According to advocates, persons with disabilities are pressured to decline treatment, even by their families, on the basis of poor quality of life (as perceived by others).

The right to decline treatment. There are periods in the history of psychiatry when doctors imposed treatments like electroshock therapy and lobotomies, with family consent, but in opposition to the patient's choice.

The right to die. Ending life voluntarily is controversial. Physician-assisted suicide is not legal in most states. Advocates think there is pressure to end life for the wrong reasons. People with incurable and progressively worsening illnesses can live for decades with the right assistance.

Right to accommodation and treatment as social justice. Is medical care a right "at any cost?" Our laws require reasonable accommodation, but they do not define the boundaries on medical treatment – how much treatment is a moral and feasible right.

Now, bioethical decisions are informed and influences by the perspective of persons with disabilities. Documents such as "The Right to Live and To Be Different" express views that were not well known before the disability rights movement.

SLIDE 17:

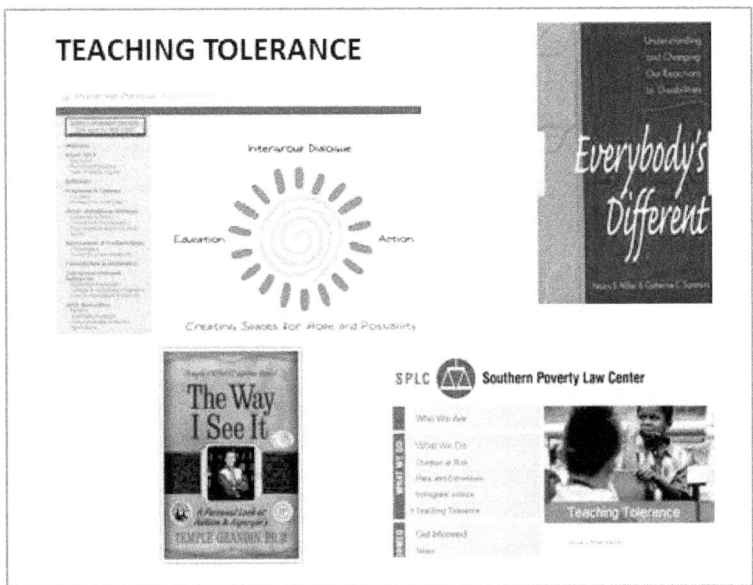

The **entertainment media** can, with intention, change and "undo" prejudice and stereotypes. This was demonstrated in the program Sesame Street for children, launched in 1969.

Movies such as the **biography of Dr. Temple Grandin** in 2010 dispel the mystery and fear of Impairments such as **autism.**

There are learning experiences designed to **raise unconscious emotional reactions and assumptions**, and change them. There is a book on the subject written by a psychologist and a psycho-therapist that offers a model for addressing deep assumptions bound up with emotions.

Undergraduates can be educated in difference and diversity through a model called **Intergroup Dialog**, which is one course offering.

There are many other "**curriculums for tolerance**," for children and adults, for example, from the **Southern Poverty Law Center.**

The **implicit bias tests** that are available online from Harvard University help convince people that they have unconscious biases.

We have learned much about unconscious bias and discrimination and how to reduce it, whether pertaining to gender, race, ethnicity, or disability. A number of approaches have worked, although they are not widely known or widely used: legal pressures to stop discrimination, social marketing, special education, representations in the entertainment media, and specially designed educational workshops.

SLIDE 18:

See pictoral history of disability at http://www.hss.state.ak.us/gcdse/history/HTML_Content_Main.htm

The roots of discrimination can be found in the early history of Western civilization. Societies and cultures have struggled with the fact that some people are going to be disabled. The worst treatments were responses to severe intellectual impairments and extreme deformation, especially in children.

Ancient beliefs (Christian times, Greece, Rome) held that congenital impairments were a punishment from God or the gods. Infants were abandoned, or put to death. Some mentally deficient people were kept as slaves, for entertainment and good luck.

In the Middle Ages, there was the belief that Satan, not God, was behind severe mental impairment, including epilepsy. The Christian Church provided charity and hospices in monasteries. The English differentiated between "fools and idiots" and "lunatics." "Lunatics" could keep their property. Infirmity and poverty were part of God's varied creation—the order of things. Poor and disabled people were equally objects of charity.

During the Renaissance, medical experts studied the physical bases for impairments—hearing, vision, and the body. They experimented with treatments like beating the head, or boring a hole in the head. The English distinguished between "safe" versus "dangerous" people with mental disabilities. They also separated the "deserving" from the "undeserving" poor. Deaf people were educated in monasteries and convents. There were hospitals for the sick, elderly, and poor whose families could not care for them. Poverty in general was suspect; the poor were incarcerated. Begging was outlawed.

During the Age of Reason, idiots and madmen were differentiated. Divine punishment was questioned, as a cause. Infirmity came to be viewed in medical terms. There were alms houses, and institutions for the care of disabled and mentally ill people.

Schools for blind and deaf children were established in the 18th Century. The notion of educating "idiots" arose. However, in the American colonies, the mentally impaired were "warned out" of town, so they would not be an economic burden.

During the 19th Century, there was greater interest in treatment and cure, but also in segregating disabled people into institutions. Hospitals, asylums, workhouses, and prisons separated populations. There was worry about the need to control growing populations of the poor or "misfits" in urban centers, partially fueled by a wave of immigrants. "Special instruction" was introduced in schools, partially to protect the "normal" from the disruption of truants, non-English speaking children, and other struggling students.

People with mental illness and intellectual disability were segregated into mental hospitals. A professional cadre of caretakers managed the institutions.

There were also freak shows. Subjects were "sold" to organizers, for life, as exotic objects of entertainment.

Themes: murder of infants as "not human;" charity and hospices; lumping with poverty and crime; "punishment of God" versus exploration of medical roots and treatment; notion of education, treatment, rehabilitation; isolation into specialized institutions; rise of the rule of caretakers; protection of "normals" from scary hordes; new educational techniques for blind, deaf, mentally impaired children; public institutions assuming the burden of care.

SLIDE 19:

20TH CENTURY (pre Disability Rights Movement)

GOOD:
- Rise of psychotherapy and psychiatry
- Rise of special education, and the right to an education
- Vocational rehabilitation to bring veterans and injured workers back into workforce
- Laws aimed at helping veterans of war
- Prosthetics and better prevention – medical advances
- State assumes burden of support and regulation
- Rise of parents' advocacy; biographical writing
- Anti-psychotic drugs invented
- Better understanding of types of impairments, census

BAD
- Eugenics; fear for the purity of the human race
- Fear of immigrants and easy attribution of mental limitation
- Repression and social control over "deviants;" isolation
- Sterilization, medical experimentation, murder
- Rise of paternalism and "welfare state" mentality
- Involuntary commitment to asylums
- Isolation of disabled in institutions, over-crowding, abuses, scandals
- Poor farms become dumping grounds

GOOD:
- Rise of psychotherapy and psychiatry
- Rise of special education, and the right to an education
- Vocational rehabilitation to bring veterans and injured workers back into workforce
- Laws aimed at helping veterans of war
- Prosthetics and better prevention – medical advances
- State assumes burden of support and regulation
- Rise of parents advocacy; biographical writing
- Anti-psychotic drugs invented
- Better understanding of types of impairments, census

BAD
- Eugenics; fear for the purity of the human race
- Fear of immigrants and easy attribution of mental limitation
- Repression and social control over "deviants"
- Sterilization, medical experimentation, murder
- Rise of paternalism and "welfare state" mentality
- Involuntary commitment to asylums
- Isolation of disabled in institutions, over-crowding, abuses, scandals
- Poor farms become dumping grounds

Eugenicists built on fears about the links between physical and mental impairments and social evils such as crime and unemployment. They succeeded in introducing forced sterilization programs in England and in the U.S. There were about 47,000 sterilizations in 30 states between 1907 and 1949. The Supreme Court affirmed the states' right to sterilize for a period during that time.

Repression and social control was seen as the way to limit the "contamination" of the race.

The Nazis sterilized up to 400,000 people in Germany and put nearly as many to death.

Shock therapy was introduced as a cure for mental illness in the 1920s. Psychosurgery (such as lobotomies) were used after 1933. In the U.S., a law gave patients the right to refuse electroshock treatment. Patients in asylums were subject to medical experiments.

The modern idea of rehabilitation was a byproduct of World War I. Many men survived the war with impairments and needed to be re-assimilated into society.

An industry of professional caretakers developed, to run institutions, rehab programs, and special education. Disability became a concern of the state.

Psychiatrists increasingly used anti-psychotic drugs rather than psychotherapy to treat mental illness.

The late 20th Century saw the rise of the disability rights movement, the independent living movement, and community-based support. Historical oppression and exclusion was challenged internationally.

Disability Studies as an academic field grew. Assistive technologies flourished as an industry especially after World War II. National standards for accessibility and accommodation were developed.

SLIDE 20:

Universal Design is a set of guidelines for designing everyday products for wider range of people, including both older and younger persons with impairments.

National standards are evolving to address a wide range of accommodations for people who have impairments. These accommodations also help a large number of people in the population considered "able-bodied," depending on situational circumstances, for example, parent who need to carry or move children, people pulling luggage or pulling loading carts, people who are temporarily ill, injured, or distracted.

SLIDE 21:

> **PEOPLE-FIRST LANGUAGE**
>
> **The language used to discuss disability is emotionally charged.**
>
> - Use "person or people with disabilities" and not "handicapped," "crippled," or "the impaired."
> - Use "person with a cognitive disability," not "idiot," "imbecile," "feeble-minded," "mentally retarded," "moron," "mentally defective," or "Mongoloid."
> - The preferred language is "person-first" language.
>   It asks that you see the person first.
>   It counters the tendency to see the impairment first, e.g., "the blind."
> - An **impairment** is a missing, damaged, deficient, or weakened body part or function.
> - A **disability** is the inability to perform one or more major life activities because of impairment.
>   Everyone is enabled to perform some activities by a non-disabling environment.
>   People with certain impairments can be aided to perform well with the help of people, devices, software, and architectural modifications.
>   Disability is a consequence of environment and society.

The words used to describe persons with disabilities have changed much over time and are emotionally charged.

Use **"person or people with disabilities"** and not "handicapped," "crippled," or "the impaired."

Use **"person with an intellectual disability,"** not "idiot," "imbecile," "feebleminded," "mentally retarded," "moron," "mentally defective," or "Mongoloid."

The new preferred language is **"person-first" language**. It counters the tendency to see the impairment first, e.g., "the blind." The better phrase is "person who is blind" or "blind person."

Impairment is a missing, damaged, deficient, or weakened body part or function.

A **disability** is a difficulty or the inability to perform one or more major life activities because of impairment, under usual conditions. Everyone is enabled to perform activities **by a non-disabling environment**; people with certain impairments can be aided to perform well in typically-designed environments with the help of people, devices, software, and architectural modifications. **Thus disability is a consequence of environment and society in relation to specific personal characteristics.**

Given a long history of mistreatment and negative labeling, **"there is no neutral language with which to discuss disability."**

One theory is that groups that are ostracized replace the names referring to them nearly every generation, to erase the slur that accrues to a current name, until they feel they have reached an era of respect.

SLIDE 22:

> **STIGMA**
>
> - A mark of shame and disgrace
> - People who do not have "ordinary and normal" characteristics re stigmatized
> - Stigma "spoils the social identity;" it is a form of "social death"
> - It disrupts every social interaction
> - People are stigmatized for violating social norms
> - Western civilizations prize personal autonomy, independence
> - Disabled people are constant reminders of the "negative body"—which the able-bodied are trying to avoid, forget, and ignore
>
> *STIGMA: NOTES ON THE MANAGEMENT OF SPOILED IDENTITY by ERVING GOFFMAN*
>
> Erving Goffman, Stigma, 1963
> L.M.C. Brown, 2010
> L. Colman, 2006

Erving Goffman introduced the word "stigma" to describe the phenomenon or exclusion of persons with disabilities, morally unearned. Stigma also applies to other characteristics such as race and religion that can be culturally devalued. (***Stigma**, 1963*)

During the Christian Middle Ages, criminals, slaves or traitors were tattooed, branded, or physically mutilated (including blinding) to mark them as undesirables. It was a **mark (or "stigma") of shame and disgrace**. A person with a stigma is treated by dominant groups as **sub-human, inferior**, or morally bad.

Society categorizes people as **ordinary and natural,** or not, based on certain characteristics and expectations. These categories become unconscious and automatic; they comprise a **virtual social identity**. A **person who does not have ordinary characteristics** will be perceived as tainted, bad, dangerous, or weak. These attributes **evoke stigma, or shame.**

Goffman wrote about three types of stigma. First, due to physical deformities. Second, due to qualities of character such as dishonesty, addiction, or unemployment. Finally, there are stigmas of race, nation, and religion. (We might add sexual orientation now.) **Children learn stigmas in school**, and taunt without inhibition. The **stereotypes may become specific and surprising**: for example, blind people are not supposed to make jokes, or enjoy dancing.

The central feature is social acceptance. **Stigma "spoils the social identity."** It is a form of **"social death."** The victim may internalize the stigma in self-hate. As one said, looking in a mirror, "I saw a stranger, a little, pitiable, hideous figure."

It can disrupt any social interaction. "Looking for a job was like standing before a firing squad. Employers were shocked that I had the gall to apply for a job."

[From L.M.C. Brown:]

During difficult economic times, there is increased aggression and more toward stigmatized groups. "Some people are stigmatized for violating norms, whereas **others are stigmatized for being of little economic or political value**."

Not all "otherness" or "difference" is stigmatized. Stigmas reflect the values of the dominant group, which determines (consciously or unconsciously) which human differences are undesired and devalued to the point of stigma.

People with disabilities may be constant reminders of the "**negative body**" – what many able-bodied are trying to avoid, forget, and ignore.

Western civilizations prize personal autonomy and independence. Dependence and helplessness is associated with being child-like. Women are expected to be attractive. Adults should have children. Negative cultural views are reinforced by the media, clergy, health personnel, development agencies, and literature.

SLIDE 23:

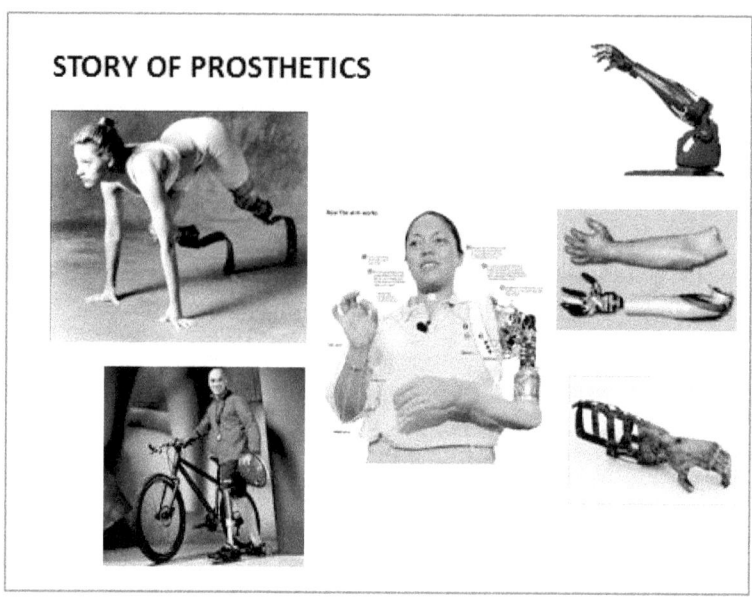

The industry in prosthetics—an application of biomedicine and computer technology -- has grown particularly in response to wounded veterans.

Advanced prosthetics are making recent war veterans more mobile than previous generations. Recent veterans are likely to be re-assimilated into society and able to participate in more activities than ever (e.g., hand controls on cars). There is a new wave of amputees, whether or not veterans, participating in sports and enjoying specialized sports equipment (e.g., using bikes driven by hand-cranks for paraplegics, special skis, legs that support running).

After WW II, public media featured the American Worker in contrast with Europeans. The new "icons of American labor" were pictured as masculine, independent, reliable, efficient, and resilient. Industrial production helped win the war. The blue-collar worker was a hero and represented American vigor and promise.

At the same time, veterans were returning who were wounded, disfigured, or traumatized. The media portrayed brave amputees who came back to get married, buy a house, get an education, and join the workforce. Patriotism, pride, and victory were linked to disability and masculinity. Disability—represented as post-war amputees—became a symbol of sacrifice and patriotism.

An industry in prostheses flourished, fixing the "damaged male body." New materials were found, and bioengineering emerged as a field.

New artificial arms and legs represented a new body-machine interface for amputees and made it possible for them to look and act like "normal, able-bodied working men." Amputees were linked to cutting edge scientific and engineering invention. There were acrylic eyes, dental prostheses, acrylic facial parts, and electrically controlled artificial limbs and cybernetic arms.

The labor market was, however, biased toward the physically fit and robust, with a value on high productivity.

Public images of amputees assured the public that they had suffered no loss of ability, personality, or manhood. They were "normal."

Ironically, the development of cybernetic arms led to the development of industrial robots and robotic arms. Robotics began to displace manual workers in large-scale manufacturing and industrial production by the mid-1960s. The purposes of rehabilitating amputees to turn them into productive laborers led to investment in the purposes of high production using robots on assembly lines.

SLIDE 24:

WHY DO WE NEED TO TAP THIS POOL OF STUDENTS?

- Participation and leadership in research and invention = better assistive technologies
- Educating all students for diversity in life experience
- Better life for all, fun, jobs
- It's fair; ability is there

Participation and leadership in research and invention

The best insights about solutions to problems of impairments are going to come from people who understand them and who care, personally.

Any product development is better if it is informed by consumers. It is even better if it is led by persons with disabilities. Assistive technologies can mean independence, freedom, dignity, and survival.

Assistive tools face an "orphan market"—small and fragmented. Commercial success is not likely. It takes personal commitment to drive the effort.

Yet the products originally designed to assist persons with disabilities have proven to have benefits to wide segments of society: elderly people, people tending children, people temporarily sick, and so on. Prosthetic arms became the basis for robotics in manufacturing plants.

Our science learned to take care of astronauts working around exotic constraints. We can improve on the quality of lives constrained by ordinary environments that were poorly designed for people with impairments.

The quality of life for everyone will benefit.

Educating all students for diversity in life experience

Our educational systems are better if they expose students to diversity, including persons with disabilities and the direct personal evidence for the potential of people with impairments to function in society and in the workplace. More students with disabilities are educated and assisted via special education, now, to participate in higher education. They provide peer examples of how to manage disabilities and how to take advantage of assistance and support services. Faculty with disabilities demonstrate that intellectual achievements and contributions can be ordinary with impairments when conditions are favorable. With 20% of the population having some impairment, and 85% of impairments acquired later in life, the odds are that everyone is exposed to the issues personally. The opportunities for persons with disabilities are changing dramatically, and we need more people to understand what is available and possible.

SLIDE 25:

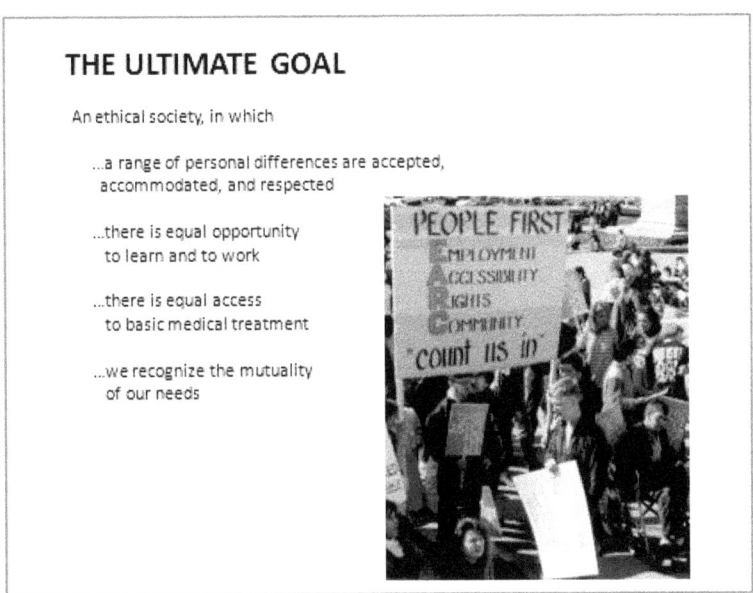

The goals of the disability rights movement are the same as those of any other group that is treated with "difference" and "subordination."

The goal is an ethical society and civilization in which a wide range of personal differences are accepted and accommodated, and every person is treated with respect and given equal opportunity. We hold a philosophy of mutuality of need and responsiveness to the needs of all individuals in our society.

Social Darwinism gave us the view that species and people were in competition for survival, and the fittest won. Those who are "unfit" are discards and failures, to be pushed aside. The new view, regarding disability, is that many impairments can be "made fit" through accommodation and assistance. The biggest barrier to the "fitness" of many individuals (including persons with disabilities, women, racial and ethnic minorities) is a societal view that deems them worthy of stigma, harassment, suppression, oppression, and neglect.

International policy and American policy and laws are increasingly affirming our need to accept individual rights to life, to equal opportunity and access to education, to basic medical treatment, and to respect.

SLIDE 26

The Center for Assistive Technology and Environmental Access (CATEA) at Georgia Tech is an example of comprehensive efforts to develop and support assistive technologies.

There are four laboratories:
1. Rehabilitation Engineering and Applied Research Laboratory (REAR)
2. Accessible Workplace Laboratory
3. Enabling Environments Laboratory (EE)
4. Accessible Education and Information Laboratory

Engineers, scientists, clinicians, and others are drawn from the Georgia Tech College of Architecture and other universities, the U.S. Veteran's Administration, and centers. They conduct research and teach courses, for example, in prosthetics and orthotics.

There are clusters of information organized for students, professionals in the field, consumers, and inventors.

The Accessible Education and Information Laboratory provides information on education and technology, with a special focus on the accessibility of distance education for students with disabilities.

Current special projects are providing:
- information for university instructors who teach people with disabilities,
- guidance for high school teachers on making science, engineering, and math classrooms and labs accessible,

- a national public web site on assistive technology
- a network of older and younger people with disabilities to test prototypes, products and services designed for them
- Georgia Tech Research on Accessible Distance Education, tutorials and tools for creating accessible distance learning

SCIENCE AND ENGINEERING EDUCATION AND THE PARTICIPATION OF PERSONS WITH DISABILITIES

The problems of impairment can and should be solved by people with disabilities. They need to be among the leaders in research and design.

—T. Shakespeare

WHY IS INCLUSION IMPORTANT?

The design of assistive technologies is better with the input, insight, and leadership of people for whom it is being created.

Until recently, national policies that focused on the needs of people with disabilities have tended to concentrate on health and benefits, and not on science and technology.[2] Understandably, the needs of accessibility compete with attention to national security, space, energy, and health. The economic weight of assistive technologies is not clear. But for quality of life, we know that developing assistive technologies, and making consumer products, telecommunications, and transportation accessible, is important.

For persons with disabilities who benefit from assistive technologies, the impact is potentially a matter of survival, freedom, and independence. Their motivation as designers is high.

New products support independent living, community integration, learning and work. The idea of universal design – "all products and all environments are usable to the greatest extent possible by people of all ages and abilities" – is an unmet goal. Our society is just beginning to acknowledge that there is a range of different abilities, and many are not, but could, be accommodated. We are learning more about how discrimination poses a

---

[2] Seelman, K.D. (2001). Is disability a missing factor? In G. Albrecht, K. Seelman & M. Bury (Eds.), *Handbook of disability studies* (pp. 663-692). Thousand Oaks, CA: Sage.

barrier to accommodation. There is no single consumer voice in the marketplace for assistive technologies, which makes it harder to convey the message. The marketplace for assistive technology products is fragmented by various disability subgroups and the variety of products that meet their needs (for example, hearing aids, voice-activated software, robotic limbs).

Because of fragmentation and small markets, the field is sometimes called orphan technology. Commercial revenue and funding are problems. Although the products can benefit a broad range of consumers, they are unlikely to reach the level of mass market sales.

The science establishment does not want to engage in "identity politics" whereby a person's group is a factor in their recruitment and intellectual performance, but the sociology of science shows patterns of exclusion of certain groups. If we agree that science (and technology) is a social system, reflecting social values and structures, then we can explain why certain topics rise to prominence over others, and how the education of scientists may or may not encourage social responsibility and interest in solving socially-relevant problems. Cross-culturally, the sociology of science shows patterns of exclusion of certain groups from the enterprise of science (women, minorities, and persons with disabilities) in the U.S.. This hinders the objective pursuit of solutions that might benefit an excluded minority.

Values do influence where we invest. Sympathy for disabled veterans, for example, has driven trends in engineering. Post World War II, the emphasis on investment was on the rehabilitation of disabled veterans. Medical rehabilitation and rehabilitation engineering flourished, especially in the development of prosthetics (artificial body parts) and orthotics (supports for weakened limbs). Later research looked at wheel chairs, hearing aids, and Braille printers.

The introduction of products can disturb social and psychological identity, and the participation of the consumer can mitigate that effect. The invention of particular products can trigger unintended consequences in raising false hopes, for example, or disturbing identity based on certain impairment. For example, the Functional Electronic Stimulator (FES) uses electronic stimulation to activate nerves affected by paralysis resulting from spinal cord injury, stroke, or head injury. It can restore limb and organ function, allowing people with paralysis to walk and to awaken the brain from a coma. For deaf people, a cochlear implant can mean dissociation from deaf "manualists" who take pride in their culture.

We need cultural sensitivity in the development of assistive technologies. The trend in modern technology development is to value the input and feedback from the consumer of a product. Finding people who understand both the disability and the technical design process is challenging. The disability rights movement, from the 1960s on, challenged decision-making about treatments, devices, and services without the participation of the consumer --people with disabilities. Advocates point to the need for developing assistive technology but with cultural sensitivity and participation, in making decisions about what devices are needed, how they are designed, and how they are tested.

There is already recognition for the value of inclusion, and there needs to be more. After 1980, U.S. science and technology policy was strongly tied to the economy, national innovation and competitiveness. At the same time, Federal programs supported efforts to recruit women, minorities, and persons with disabilities to the workforce. A National Institute on Disability and Rehabilitation Research (NIDRR) was founded in 1978 to lead assistive technology policy and R&D. It supports 14 centers and a technology deployment program under the Assistive Technology Act of 1988. Its New Scholars Program has recruited a number of disabled students.

The development of international technical standards was helped by the Rehabilitation Engineering Society of North America (RESNA) established in 1979. Later in 1997, the Association of Access Engineering Specialists (AAES) formed to facilitate dialog between the disability community and industry. These professional associations serve as development partners and consumers.

Standards for wheel chairs and the computer interface called the World Wide Web were developed through international initiatives with formal participation of consumers.

People with disabilities have been excluded from participation in society, and excluded from the organizations and services designed to help them. The most appropriate solutions to problems of impairment should be solved with leadership by disabled people. "Research accountable to, and preferably done by, disabled people offers the best insights" into disability.[3]

---

[3] Shakespeare, T. (2010). The social model of disability. In L.J. Davis (Ed.), *The disability studies reader* (3rd Ed.) (pp. 266-273). New York: Routledge.

INCLUSION IS NATIONAL GOAL

It is a national goal to increase the number of persons with disabilities in the science and engineering (S&E) workforce.[4]

The largest Federal agencies that fund research and human resource development in science and engineering (National Science Foundation, National Institutes for Health, and National Aeronautics and Space Administration) have special programs for targeted populations such as women, minorities, and persons with disabilities.

Although collecting data on this population is problematic – it is often incomplete due to under-reporting and self-reporting – data is still regularly collected and reported, as mandated by law.

There are several institutions that specialize in serving persons with disabilities: Gallaudet University (for deaf people), the National Technical Institute for the Deaf at the Rochester Institute of Technology, and Landmark College.

Programs funded by the National Science Foundation, for example, include:

- Regional Alliances for Persons with Disabilities, comprehensive research and programs based in several universities
- Facilitation Awards for Scientists and Engineers With Disabilities (FASED) supporting students and faculty to attend workshops and conferences
- Science of Learning Center on Visual Language and Visual Learning at Gallaudet
- Deaf Initiative in Technology at the National Technical Institute for the Deaf
- Universal Design in College Algebra at Landmark College

One of the challenges of serving this targeted population is that different disabilities or combinations of disability require different assistive technologies and support services. It is hard to standardize approaches.

---

[4] Committee on Equal Opportunities in Science and Engineering (2009). *Broadening participation in America's STEM workforce, 2007-2008 CEOSE Biennial Report to Congress*. CEOSE 09-01.

THE RATE OF PARTICIPATION COULD BE HIGHER

The data on students with disabilities in science and engineering are collected by the National Science Foundation.[5] The data are incomplete, because they come from students who are asked to report their own disabilities, and, there tends to be under-reporting. The extent of under-reporting is unknown.

About **11 percent of undergraduate students in a science and engineering field** have one or more disabilities, and that percentage is parallel with the number of persons with disabilities ages 15-24 in the general population. Among the latter group (people ages 15-24), *more than half (of the 11%) have learning disabilities.*

National statistics on the science and engineering workforce show that about **7 percent of graduate students in science and engineering** were persons with disabilities (in 2004, the latest year available). A greater proportion of graduate students with disabilities were women (about 57 percent). The majority were white.

Only **1 percent of people holding Ph.D.'s in science and engineering** report having disabilities.

The **number of doctorates awarded** to persons with disabilities is low (**about 1.7%**), and the absolute number has declined recently (between 1998 and 2005):

---

[5] Committee on Equal Opportunities in Science and Engineering (2009). *Broadening participation in America's STEM workforce, 2007-2008 CEOSE Biennial Report to Congress.* CEOSE 09-01. http://www.nsf.gov/od/oia/activities/ceose/index.jsp .

Table 1-5
Percent of STEM Doctoral Degrees
Awarded by Gender, Race, and Disability: 1998-2005

Group	1998	2005
Male	60.7	55.4
Female	39.3	44.6
Total	100.0 (18,271)	100.0 (16,024)
White	76.7	76.6
African American	3.5	4.4
Hispanic	4.1	5.0
American Indian/ Alaska Native	0.5	0.4
Asian/ Pacific Islander	11.8	10.2
Unknown Race/ Ethnicity	3.3	3.4
Total	100.0	100.0
Disabled Persons	1.5	1.7

Data source: Women, Minorities, and Persons with Disabilities in Science and Engineering 2007, Table F-11, U.S. Citizens and Permanent Residents; and Survey of Doctorates Earned, 1997-2006, Figure 3.

The **number of full-time faculty with disabilities in science and engineering fields** is low overall (**about 10,300**). The number of persons with disabilities in lower ranks is increasing slightly.

Table 1-8
Percent Change in Full-time STEM Faculty Positions at 4-Year Colleges
and Universities by Race and Disability: 1997 versus 2006

Group	All STEM Faculty	Professor	Associate Professor	Assistant Professor
White: 1997	120,600	57,200	35,000	28,400
2006	123,800	54,400	35,700	33,800
% Change	+3	-5	+2	+19
Black: 1997	3,800	1,200	1,300	1,300
2006	5,500	1,500	1,700	2,200
% Change	+45	+25	+31	+69
Hispanic: 1997	4,000	1,300	1,400	1,400
2006	5,400	2,100	1,600	1,700
% Change	+35	+62	+14	+21
Amer Indian.: 1997	500	300	200	100
2006	1,200	700	300	300
% Change	+140	+133	+50	+200
Asian/PI: 1997	14,100	5,200	3,700	5,200
2006	19,300	6,400	5,000	7,900
% Change	+37	+23	+35	+52
Disabled: 1997	10,300	6,300	2,900	1,100
2006	10,300	5,800	2,400	2,100
% Change	+0	-8	-17	+91

Data sources: (1997) Women, Minorities, and Persons with Disabilities, 2000, Table 5-15 and (2006) Women, Minorities, and Persons with Disabilities, 2007, Table H-25. * Black refers to African American and Native American refer to American Indian and Alaska Native. Numbers for the above three faculty groups do not add up to all faculty, because other faculty groups, e.g., instructors, are excluded from this table.

DIVERSITY IMPROVES THE QUALITY OF EDUCATION

There is clear and substantial evidence that exposing students to diverse people and views improves the quality of education. It broadens the student's sense for life experience and understanding of difference. This is true regardless of fields, but especially in those that have low numbers of diverse students such as science and engineering.[6]

The question came up clearly in 2003 in the Supreme Court's deliberation of a suit against the University of Michigan for using race-sensitive criteria in admitting students to law school and to its college. The University's intention was to ensure that it had a racially diverse student body in order to provide the best possible learning environment for students.

---

[6] American Educational Research Association, Association of American Colleges and Universities, & American Association for Higher Education (2003). *Brief of amici curiae in support of the respondents, No. 02-516, Gratz et al. v Bollinger et al.* Downloaded October 2, 2007 from http://www.vpcomm.umich.edu/admissions/legal/gra_amicus-ussc/um/AERA-gra.pdf

Many organizations supported the University's position by submitting briefs summarizing substantial research on the educational benefits of diversity. The summary of a key brief reads:

> "Research studies show that student body diversity can promote learning outcomes, democratic values and civic engagement, and preparation for a diverse society and workforce—goals that fall squarely within the basic mission of most universities. Several studies demonstrate that student body diversity broadens the range of intellectual opinions on university campuses and improves classroom learning environments that diverse learning environments promote thinking skills, and that cross-racial interaction has positive effects on retention, college satisfaction, self-confidence, interpersonal skills, and leadership. Diverse learning environments challenge students to consider alternative viewpoints and to develop tolerance for differences, and can promote participation in civic activities. Studies further show that student diversity better prepares students for an increasingly diverse workforce and society."[7]

HIGHER EDUCATION IS STILL "CHILLY"

Higher education institutions have been willing to make physical accommodations for students with disabilities. Social acceptance on the part of faculty may lag, however.[8]

Researchers interviewed ten students with disabilities at a large Midwestern university known for its support services. The group included male and female students between ages 19 to 47, with both visible (e.g., spina bifida and cerebral palsy) to invisible (e.g., learning) disabilities.

The students described incidents of impatience with the distraction of the presence of a wheel chair and physical movement, discouragement from enrolling, reluctance to

---

[7] Ibid. There is a comprehensive literature review and a web site tracking the literature.
See Smith, Daryl G. et al. (1997). *Diversity Works: the Emerging Picture of How Students Benefit*. Washington, DC: Association of American Colleges and Universities.
See Association of American Colleges and Universities and University of Maryland (2007). *DiversityWeb*. http://www.diversityweb.org/

[8] Beilke, J. R., & Yssel, N. (1999a). The chilly climate for students with disabilities in higher education. *College Student Journal, 33*(3), 364.

change the way things were taught, skepticism that the student was disabled, and denial of extra time with tests and assignments (as guidelines require for learning disabilities).

A "chilly climate" has been shown to discourage other minority students. There is devaluation of the student, through overlooking mistakes, encouraging students to switch to less rigorous majors, refusing eye contact, and generally acting in a condescending or patronizing way. Marginalized students experience lower expectations. Negative interactions with faculty and peers contribute to a system of differential treatment. The result is that students are more likely to quit the class and to dissociate themselves from the major or the field of study.

The numbers of students with disabilities entering higher education is increasing, especially after the enactment of civil rights laws that prohibit discrimination. Since the Education for All Handicapped Children Act of 1975, elementary and secondary schools are providing special education to greater numbers of students with disabilities.

In the U.S., the first college program for students with disabilities opened at the University of Illinois in 1948. However, in general, current faculty are just now encountering the large numbers of students that entered public school after 1975 and benefited from special education in larger numbers.

Learning disabilities in particular are a relatively new phenomenon, and not well understood. They are invisible. Resulting student behaviors are easily confused with lower intelligence, procrastination, poor study habits, and disorganization. Faculty can feel that academic integrity is compromised. Thirty percent more incoming freshmen have been labeled learning disabled. The rationale for labeling is not well understood, generally, and may not seem scientific to academics.

Like the reaction to affirmative action, the reaction to increasing numbers and types of students with disabilities challenges the value system and culture of higher education. Fiercely competitive faculty may find it hard to act welcoming, tolerant, and accommodating.

Early attempts to change the status of women and minorities focused on improving the abilities of individuals to compete in dominant white and male workplace.[9] This

---

[9] Schriner, K. (2001). A disability studies perspective on employment issues and policies for disabled people. In G. Albrecht, K. Seelman & M. Bury (Eds.), *Handbook of disability studies* (pp. 642-662). Thousand Oaks, CA: Sage.

approach was characterized as the "deficit model" in interventions – fix the individual by training them to look and act like the dominant group. Similarly, in the evolution of disability rights consciousness, there was an initial focus on correcting the impairments in individuals and making them "fit" the constraints of a typical education or work environment. Now we realize that the environment is unnecessarily difficult and could be improved.

The demographics of students in higher education have changed. There are more women, older students, racial and ethnic minority students, part-time students, and students with disabilities.

FRAMEWORK FOR IMPROVING ACCESS TO LEARNING

Traditional means of meeting the needs of students with disabilities included allowing extra time on tests, providing note takers, providing a sign language interpreter, and captioning on videos. They are well intended and helpful but do not add up to the effectiveness of a more systematic approach. Universal Design for Instruction (UDI) was developed as a comprehensive framework and a set of principles, to guide new ways to teach.[10]

UDI's foundation is Universal Design which originated in the field of architecture. Universal Design identifies features of products and environments that anticipate a variety of needs, ages, abilities, and disabilities. Many of those features benefit everyone, for example curb cuts on sidewalks make navigation easier for people with strollers, luggage, loading carts, and bicycles, as well as wheelchairs.

Like Universal Design, Universal Design for Instruction starts with principles and then translates those principles into concrete actions, into the design of courses and the initiation of beneficial approaches in the classroom:[11]

1. **Equitable use:**
    - Design instruction for students with diverse abilities, for example, provide class notes and make them accessible regardless of hearing ability, English proficiency, learning or attention disorders, or note-taking skills.

---

[10] Scott, S., McGuire, J.M., & Embry, P. (2002). *Universal design for instruction fact sheet*. Storrs: University of Connecticut, Center on Postsecondary Education and Disability.

[11] Scott, S., McGuire, J.M., & Shaw, S.F. (2003). Universal design for instruction: a new paradigm for adult instruction in postsecondary education. *Remedial and Special Education*, 24, 6 (November/December), 369-379.

2. **Flexibility in use:**
   - Design instruction to accommodate a wide range of abilities. Provide choice in methods. For example, transfer information through lectures with visuals, group activities, use of stories, web-based discussions.
3. **Simple and intuitive:**
   - Simplify instructions and expectations; eliminate complexity. For example, explain the basis for grading, provide a syllabus, and guide students through homework assignments.
4. **Perceptible information:**
   - Anticipate different sensory abilities. For example, select materials that have digital versions as an alternative to paper copy, as they can be accessed using tools such as screen readers and text enlargers.
5. **Tolerance for error:**
   - Anticipate different paces of learning and different foundations in pre-requisite skills. For example, allow for breaking up a large assignment into smaller pieces for incremental feedback and provide online practice exercises that supplement classroom instruction.
6. **Low physical effort:**
   - Unless physical effort is integral to the course, minimize it. For example, allow the use of word processors for those who have difficulty with handwriting.
7. **Size and space for approach and use:**
   - Organize the physical setting so that body size, mobility, movement, and reach are not limitations. For example, use a circular seating arrangement so that students can see the instructor.
8. **A community of learners:**
   - Promote interaction among students and between students and faculty. For example, foster study groups, email lists, chat rooms. Make personal connection with students, encouraging them and acknowledging excellent performance.
9. **Instructional climate:**
   - Make the learning experience welcoming and inclusive. Have high expectations for all students. For example, affirm the need for peer respect and an expectation of tolerance. Encourage students to discuss special needs with the instructor. Highlight role models for contributions to the field. Recognize creative approaches on the part of students in the class.

ORIGINS OF UNIVERSAL DESIGN OF INTRUCTION (UDI)

Disability services in higher education evolved and expanded in the 1980s and 1990s, following the Education for All Handicapped Children Act (1975) and the Americans with Disabilities Act (1990).[12] The demographics of college students changed: more students with disabilities entered college.

The instructional environment of the K-12 system, subject to the Education for All law and its successor (IDEA in 2004), is quite different.[13] Teachers must be certified and must continually maintain their professional skills as educators. There are specialists in the education of children with disabilities, with certification for the specialty. K-12 students are assured access to schooling by law. The curriculum is standardized at the state level. By contrast, students are not assured a postsecondary education. Colleges are not obligated to provide a special curriculum and services. Standardization of any curriculum on a state or national level is unlikely. Faculty are not expected to be experts in pedagogy, but rather research and scholarship in an academic field. The reward system minimizes the importance of teaching and ways to improve it.

UDI was just introduced in 1998, following focus groups with college faculty and incorporating research on faculty development and approaches to college instruction. There was pressure for accountability from the American Association for Higher Education.[14]

SUPPORT TO FACULTY FOR UDI

There are a number of centers and websites serving faculty, especially junior faculty and graduate teaching assistants, as they seek to assimilate and incorporate principles of Universal Design for Instruction.

The University of Connecticut's Center on Postsecondary Education and Disability offers information about the UDI principles and is collecting descriptions of instructional products and methods put into practice.[15]

---

[12] McGuire, J.M. & Scott, S.S. (2006). Universal design for instruction: extending the Universal Design paradigm to college instruction. *Journal of Postsecondary Education and Disability*, 19:2, 124-132.

[13] Ibid., p. 126.
[14] Ibid. p. 126.
[15] University of Connecticut, Center on Postsecondary Education and Disability (2010). http://www.facultyware.uconn.edu

The Association on Higher Education and Disability (AHEAD) offers standards for disability services programs.[16]

An organization called CAST runs the National Center on Universal Design for Learning as of 2009, providing curriculum examples to teachers at all levels, as well as technical assistance, online and in-person courses, and resource materials.[17]

The University of Washington's DO-IT project houses The Faculty Room, a concentration of materials for faculty and administrators: videos showing accommodation strategies, sample PowerPoint presentations to be used to educate others about accessibility, videos showing students with particular disabilities and how they use assistive tools, an online course for faculty on the topic, explanation of legal issues, FAQs and case studies.[18]

There is at least one project focused on teachers and faculty specifically teaching science and engineering courses.[19] SciTrain, at the Center for Assistive Technology and Environmental Access (CATEA) at Georgia Tech, is conducting research in methods to train high school math and science teachers to be more effective instructors for students with disabilities. It is identifying accommodations currently made in classrooms, and identifying accommodations needed. It provides online training modules that teachers can use for students with disabilities, specifically in courses in science, computer science, and mathematics.

In parallel, SciTrain U provides tools for postsecondary educators to implement Universal Design for Learning principles in the collage classroom.[20] It offers a tutorial called "Accessible STEM Teaching 101" designed "to answer many of the questions instructors raise who have never taught a student with a disability." It also offers "Improved Teaching for Large Lecture Classes" that is not specific to science and engineering content.

CASE STUDY IN THE RATE OF CHANGE: U OF ILLINOIS

What can we expect on the path to making accommodations to recruit and graduate more students with disabilities? Presently, there are many examples to follow and

---

[16] Association on Higher Education and Disability (2011). http://www.ahead.org/
[17] CAST (2011). http://www.cast.org and http://www.udlcenter.org
[18] University of Washington, DO-IT Project (2011). http://www.washington.edu/doit/Faculty/
[19] Georgia Tech, Center for Assistive Technology and Environmental Access (CATEA)(2011). *SciTrain Project*. http://catea.gatech.edu/scitrain
[20] Ibid., http://www.catea.gatech.edu/scitrainU/login.php

build on. One historical example might serve to illustrate what is possible starting from scratch.[21] It is the story of how Tim Nugent created the University of Illinois Disability Resources and Educational Services (DRES) program.

> "From 1948 to 1960, he shepherded a program that succeeded in shattering longstanding, pervasive institutional, physical, economic, psychological, and other barriers that marginalized and ostracized people with disabilities….He battled prevalent negative social attitudes, university bureaucracy, and an inaccessible environment. He cajoled, badgered, and encouraged many students who were unprepared for postsecondary success. As a result, the Illinois program became an oasis … [for]… those considered to have the most severe impairments, including people with spinal cord injuries, post-polio disabilities, and genetic conditions such as muscular dystrophy and cerebral palsy."[22]

Several conditions set the stage and marked a shift in social values. The first national cross-disability political organization was formed in 1940. A paralyzed veterans group formed just after World War II, as did a President's Committee on the Employment of the Handicapped. There were significant incentives to veterans to reenter society and the workforce. The G.I. Bill was passed in 1944, enabling veterans to attend college with full financial support and obtain low-interest home loans.

The army built a new hospital in Galesburg, Illinois, and leased it to the University of Illinois. The hospital was ramped for wheel chair users. Here is a timeline of events:

1948   Students enter the program: 8 wheel-chair users and 5 semi-ambulatory students (all veterans)

Next semester, 3 non-veterans and a female wheelchair user enter

1949   The state threatens to close it, but a protest and a technicality save the day.

The program is moved to the Urbana campus, with 14 students.

Six classroom buildings are ramped. Elevator use is provided.

---

[21] Brown, Steven E. (2008). Breaking barriers: the pioneering disability students services program at the University of Illinois, 1948-1960. In Tamura, E. (Ed.), The history of discrimination in U.S. education: marginality, agency, and power. New York: Palgrave Macmillan, 165-192.
[22] Ibid. p. 165.

Nugent introduces wheelchair basketball and a tournament, which helps publicize DRES.

1950   22 students are enrolled

U of Illinois becomes the first university to put in curb cuts to accommodate students with disabilities.

1952   Greyhound donates buses fitted with hydraulic lifts.

Classes (up to 60-70) are moved to accessible buildings if needed, for students in the program.

1953   The university requires that all future buildings be designed for accessibility. This is a first for any university. New dormitories have accessible showers and toilets.

A service fraternity of male and female students with disabilities incorporates and helps with resolving problems, and promotes a social life.

1954   Students invite the governor of Illinois to give a keynote speech, and he "packs the house."

Services include: counseling (all kinds), preregistration, coordination of all services, three hours of individual physical instruction and therapy.

38 students graduate and find employment.

A Student Rehabilitation Center is created. Two buses provide transportation.

1955   More than 100 students from 20 states are in the program; a quota is set for 120.

The housing facility is remodeled. Parking is provided.

1958   61 additional ramps are installed into university buildings.

Students represent 25 states.

1960   Students experience a 100% placement rate on graduation.

1964   Over 1000 students had participated, and 307 graduated.

Many of the entering students led sheltered and protected lives until their DRES experience. Nugent required a "functional training week" which was an orientation and a test of abilities. He believed that students needed to be hardened for the world after school. Students in wheelchairs were expected to push themselves, climb in and out of bed, and bathe independently.

The DRES program at the University of Illinois Urbana became a model for other universities. The directors went on to assist others in building similar programs. Many universities have similar programs now which are being expanded into more specialized services, for example, focusing on particular curriculum areas such as science and engineering, and taking full advantage of assistive technologies.

EXPERIENCE WITH SUCCESSES

Students with learning disabilities who receive comprehensive support as students are able to develop strategies to compensate for difficulties due to their disability.[23]

Some of the difficulties students with disabilities include: difficulty processing information (understand spoken or writing material), retention (remember content), complete tasks in the amount of time allotted, and perception (reversing numbers or letters).

Compensations include spending extra time to do work, asking for assistance and clarification, and monitoring work for errors.

Studies of employment of persons with learning disabilities show mixed results: both problems in obtaining and maintaining jobs, and, success. Some of the variables that explain the mixed results are: socioeconomic status, differences in intellectual ability, differences in family support, and educational intervention. It is important to note that the severity and type of difficulty varies under the label of "learning disability," as does a student's history in educational and social support.

A key variable is whether the adult has learned to understand his or her own areas of strength, and chosen employment and a career that leverage strengths and avoid weaknesses. For example, students who are good at visual-perceptual and quantitative information will enter engineering, accounting, and finance. Those with reading disorders will avoid positions that emphasize reading and writing reports. Students with learning

---

[23] Adelman, P. B., & Vogel, S. A. (1990). College Graduates with Learning Disabilities: Employment Attainment and Career Patterns. *Learning Disability Quarterly, 13*(3), 154-166.

disabilities go into law and engineering, for example, but may have to work harder than others, and, learn where to pay extra attention.

The numbers of students with this disability increased dramatically as a result of the Rehabilitation Act of 1973. Support programs offer early diagnostic evaluation, remediation, coordination with faculty and tutors, and advising. This intervention has proven to have long-term benefits to the students. Self-awareness and adoption of special strategies can compensate for the learning disability, and help the student choose career paths and jobs that maximize their success.

LAWS MANDATE ACCOMMODATION

Higher education as an employer is subject to the same laws as any other. An employer may not ask when, where, or how a candidate was injured.[24] He can legally ask if an accommodation is needed, and what type. He may ask the candidate to describe or demonstrate how they would perform the job with or without an accommodation.

Candidates for employment do not have to disclose a medical condition unless they will need a reasonable accommodation.

Reasonable accommodations include:

- Written materials in accessible formats such as large print, Braille, or electronic form
- Extra time to complete a test
- Physical access to recruitment fairs, interviews, tests, and training
- Modified equipment or devices (computer for blind person, telephone access for deafness, a glare guard, one-handed keyboard, etc.)
- Physical modifications in the workspace
- Permission to work from home
- Leave for treatment, recuperation, or training
- Modified or part-time work schedule
- A job coach

---

[24] U.S. Equal Employment Opportunity Commission (2008). *Veterans with service-connected disabilities in the workplace and the Americans With Disabilities Act (ADA).* Downloaded on August 2, 2010 from http://www.eeoc.gov/facts/veterans-disabilities.html

- Reassignment to a vacant position if the current one is not workable with reasonable accommodation

SUCCESSFUL SCIENTISTS AND ENGINEERS WITH DISABILITIES

There were over 20,000 persons with disabilities in faculty positions in science and engineering fields in 2006. Every one of them probably has a story of struggle with some impairment, navigating social stigmas and discrimination, and benefiting from unique supports and assistance, alongside the challenges of professional preparation and performance.

Some well-known scientists and inventors (as well as national leaders) had disabilities that were hidden or undiagnosed. They demonstrate the potential for achievement in spite of impairments, and how societal views might be the biggest barrier.

The point of success stories is to celebrate success in spite of the odds, to present role models – people who are professionally successful, who might in some cases have made a particular contribution *because of having a certain disability or being exposed to a family member with one.* Their examples remind us of the realities of disability in the context of professions (e.g., science and engineering) that we stereotype as "hard" and "inaccessible" even for able-bodied individuals.

HISTORICAL EXAMPLES

The physicist **Stephen Hawking** has had Lou Gehrig's disease for 26 years. He can no longer speak and can barely move. With his technological and social support, he functions as a professor of physics at Cambridge University. He has the help of family, three nurses, and a graduate student. "His talent had been developed and recognized before he fell seriously ill."[25]

Robert Murphy was a professor of anthropology at Columbia University. At the age of 52 in 1976, he was diagnosed as having a tumor of the spinal cord. It caused progressive paralysis. About ten years later (1987) he published *The Body Silent* about the experience

---

[25] Wendell, S. (2010). Toward a feminist theory of disability. In L.J. Davis (Ed.), *The disability studies reader* (3rd Ed.) (pp. 336-352). New York: Routledge.

of disability from an anthropological view, while continuing his teaching and research until his death in 1990.[26]

Louis Braille, the inventor of Braille (embossed symbols that enable reading by blind people), became blind after he accidentally stabbed himself in the eye with his father's awl. [27]

Sabriye Tenberken co-founded Braille Without Borders, a non-profit educating blind students in Tibet. She became gradually visually impaired and completely blind by the age of thirteen due to retinal disease. She studied Mongolian, Chinese, and Tibetan languages and developed a Tibetan Braille script. (Disabled World source)

Dr. Jacob Bolotin was the first congenitally blind man to receive a medical license, at the turn of the 20th Century. He advocated for the full inclusion of blind people in education, employment, and all other aspects of society. Awards named for him are presented each year by the National Federation of the Blind. (DW)

Bernard Morin is a French mathematician, especially a topologist. He has been blind since age 6, but his blindness did not prevent him from having a successful career in mathematics. (DW)

Albert Einstein was known to suffer from dyslexia mainly because of his bad memory and his constant failure to memorize the simplest of things. He would not remember the months in the year. He may have never learned how to properly tie his shoelaces. It is also thought that he had OCD. Some characteristics may indicate that Einstein had Asperger's. He could not speak fluently at the age of nine, and language delays are common in children with high functioning autism. His parents suspected that he might actually be mentally retarded. At the ceremony of induction as an American, Einstein attended without socks. Frequently, children with Asperger's struggle with finding socks that feel right or with a line at the toe that does not bother them. (DW)

---

[26] Murphy, Robert (1995). Encounters: The body silent in America. In B. Ingstad & S.R. Whyte (Eds.), *Disability and culture* (pp. 140-158). Berkeley: University of California Press. Originally published in 1987.

[27] Disabled World (2006). Well known people with disabilities. Downloaded on August 3, 2010 from http://www.disabled-world.com/artman/publish/article_0060.shtml The Disabled World web site provides many short biographies of historically important people with alleged disabilities. "DW" denotes this source.

Alexander Graham Bell invented the telephone in an attempt to find a way that could make deaf people hear. His mother was slowly becoming deaf when Alexander was only 12 years old. He himself had dyslexia which would cause him problems at school. He co-founded the National Geographic society. (DW)

Leonardo Da Vinci was a Tuscan polymath: scientist, mathematician, engineer, inventor, anatomist, painter, sculptor, architect, botanist, musician and writer. He had dyslexia. Most of the time, he wrote his notes backwards. (DW)

In school, the young **Thomas Edison's** mind often wandered. He was noted to be terrible at mathematics, unable to focus, and had difficulty with words and speech. This ended Edison's three months of official schooling. The cause of Edison's deafness has been attributed to a bout of scarlet fever during childhood and recurring untreated middle ear infections. Thomas Edison was dyslexic. He was not well-coordinated and did poorly in sports. (DW)

John Horner is one of the most well known paleontologists in the United States. His dyslexia precluded a college degree, which was not diagnosed until he was an adult and had not graduated from college. While working at Princeton he went to a diagnostic center, and his dyslexia was formally diagnosed. "I wasn't diagnosed until well after I had reached adulthood, had struggled through school being considered lazy, dumb, and perhaps even retarded, and had flunked out of college seven times." (DW)

Alfred Nobel was a Swedish chemist, engineer, innovator, armaments manufacturer and the inventor of dynamite. He was subject to migraines and convulsions from infancy. Nobel had epileptic seizures as a young child. (DW)

Michelangelo's attention was constantly on his art work and he suffered from Obsessive Compulsive Disorder. He was not a social person and had a short temper which would often blow to anger inside normal conversations with family members or strangers. He would avoid people most of the time and sometimes would even walk out of a conversation for no apparent reason. When an opinion would offend his beliefs he would get angry and simply leave. Michelangelo was also known for always sleeping in his clothes including even his boots. He would almost never remove his boots even when they would cause damage to his feet. He would isolate himself for long periods of time working on himself and his arts, while ignoring and showing no emotion towards his surroundings. There was no doubt that Michelangelo had suffered from OCD. (DW)

Charles Darwin possibly had OCD and stuttered. Darwin stated that his health problems began as early as 1825 when he was only sixteen years old, and became incapacitating around age 28. The exact nature of his illnesses remains mysterious at this time. (DW)

Nikola Tesla was an inventor, physicist, mechanical engineer, and electrical engineer. He was a germophobe, hated touching round objects, disliked hair other than his own, found jewelry repulsive, and tended to do things that were either in 3's or in numbers divisible by 3. For meals he insisted on estimating the mass of everything he was about to consume, always used 18 napkins, and refused to eat alone with a woman. (DW)

Isaac Newton dropped out of school as a teenager. A person with Asperger's may not be able to accept rules in school if they appear illogical, pursuing a point or argument as a matter of principle, which can lead to a significant conflict with teachers and school authorities. (DW)

Benjamin Franklin's peers did not give him the assignment of writing the Declaration of Independence because they feared that he would conceal a joke in it. People with Asperger's are notorious for an extreme or different sense of humor. (DW)

CONTEMPORARIES

At a workshop in 2009, a number of presenters shared their personal stories:[28]

Bill McCarthy is a professor of civil engineering at New Mexico State University, injured in a car accident 43 years ago, and uses a wheel chair.

David Wohlers is a professor of chemistry at Truman State University. He lost sight in one eye at age 4 and in the other at age 8. He uses a device called a Perkins Brailler to convert English text to Braille.

Ian Shipsey is a professor of physics at Purdue University. He lost his hearing in 1989, as a side effect of cancer treatment. "I was hired with excellent hearing. … I could not work for two years. I learned to lip read. … For the next 12 years as a faculty member, I used lip-reading to communicate. … [At large physics meetings] it is impossible to lip-read. .. I developed a close-knit group of graduate students. We did research one-on-one so I

---

[28] *Report from the workshop of excellence empowered by a diverse academic workforce: chemists, chemical engineers, and materials scientists with disabilities.* February 2009, Arlington VA

could lip-read with each of them. Many of them were foreign. Many of them did not speak English well. … So I took them." Twelve years after he became deaf, he got a cochlear implant. At the end of his first semester teaching he was awarded Purdue Physics Professor of the Year based on student votes.

Victor Day is a director of the Small Molecule X-ray Crystallography and Protein Structure Laboratories at the University of Kansas. He was diagnosed with rapid cycling bipolar disorder over 15 years ago. Medication has controlled his symptoms. "When I was diagnosed, I was relieved. … I'd go off on somebody for no apparent reason, a minor thing, reduce them to tears…. There are a lot of people that have these types of disabilities—who go through cycles—and they probably aren't even aware of it. If they're depressed they'll stay out of the department a while. If they're manic—and if they're smart—they'll stay out of the department then, too. But they usually don't."

"PROBLEM SOLVERS" INSPIRATION

A group of scientists and engineers gathered at a meeting in 2009 to highlight how professionals with disabilities have "solved the problems" of navigating their work environments alongside succeeding as professional scientists, engineers, technologists, and mathematicians.[29] Fifty individuals with paraplegia, neurodegenerative diseases, hearing loss, blindness, as well as invisible disabilities such as attention deficit hyperactivity disorder, Asperger's syndrome, and poor health, attended and described how they found a way to build satisfying, high-impact careers. Some of their challenges included difficulties with the logistics or travel, and old building structures with inaccessible bathrooms. Trends like the increased use of email were a boon to someone whose hearing diminished. These types of accounts help increase our awareness of the conditions of disability , awareness of the range of assistive technologies that are in routine use, and our perceptions of the potential of individuals with disabilities in science and engineering careers.

GOAL

In summary, persons with disabilities represent an under-utilized talent pool available to enhance the U.S. economic competitiveness and innovation in science and engineering. They are a source of talent for contributions to discovery and innovation, and particularly for improving the quality of life for everyone through the design of new and

---

[29] American Association for the Advancement of Science (2010, January 27). Engineers with disabilities describe creative, persistent strategies they took to succeed [Press release]. Retrieved from http://www.aaas.org/news/releases/2010/0127problem_solvers.shtml

better assistive products. The barriers of discrimination and lack of accommodation stand in the way, and can be removed with intention.

A SHORT READER AND SYLLABUS FOR DISABILITY STUDIES

Outline

- People-First Language
- What is a Disability? Who is Disabled?
- How Many People Have Disabilities?
- Historical Timeline
- The Disability Rights Movement
- Is the Disability Rights Movement Similar to the Civil Rights and Women's Rights Movements?
- What is the Experience of Persons With Disabilities?
- Discrimination and Treatment of Persons With Disabilities
- Special Education
- Learning Disabilities
- Universal Design
- Assistive Technology (AT)

People-First Language

> *"In the United States, a controversy has raged over preferred linguistic usage: whether to use the phrase 'persons with disabilities' or 'disabled people.'"*
>
> -G.D. Albrecht, K.D. Seelman & M. Bury

SENSITIVITIES

The words used to describe persons with disabilities have changed much over time and are emotionally very sensitive. The disability rights movement starting in the mid-20th Century rethought the labels we use.

Use "person with disabilities" and not "handicapped," "crippled," or "the impaired."

Use "person with an intellectual disability," not "idiot," "imbecile," "feebleminded," "mentally retarded," "moron," "mentally defective," or "Mongoloid."

Use "person with deafness" or "person with blindness." Not "the deaf" or "the blind."

Why? The old words carry a lot of negative baggage, even though they are embedded in our childhood learning, literature, history, and laws.

PEOPLE-FIRST LANGUAGE

The new preferred language is called "person-first" language. It is meant to emphasize that a person has many characteristics as well as his or her impairment. It is considered more respectful to say "a person with a disability," "a man with mental retardation," or "a child with autism."

There is an analytic difference between "impairment" and "disability." "An **impairment** is a missing, damaged, deficient, or weakened body part or function." A person can have a visual impairment, or a hearing impairment, or impaired movement.

"**Disability** is the inability to perform one or more major life activities because of impairment," under usual conditions. This includes taking care of one's body, having a full range of movement, having intact senses, communicating with others, learning and working, and interacting with others socially. Whether someone is unable to perform an activity depends on the obstacles surrounding them. Obstacles can be social (the negative attitudes of others), personal (lack of information), physical (inaccessible buildings), or resources (money, training, housing). Thus disability is a consequence of environment and society in relation to specific personal characteristics.

> Miller, N. B. & Sammons, C.C. (1999). *Everybody's Different: Understanding and Changing Our Reactions to Disabilities*. Baltimore: Paul H. Brookes.

The word "disabled" does not translate easily into many languages. The social construct or identity of "disabled" is only recently being introduced into less developed countries.

> Whyte, S.R. & Ingstad, B. (1995). Disability and culture: An overview. In B. Ingstad & S.R. Whyte (Eds.), *Disability and culture* (pp. 3-34). Berkeley: University of California Press.

People with mental retardation have been called "idiot," "imbecile," "feebleminded," "moron," and "defective" at various times. Now they are "persons with mental retardation" or "persons with developmental disabilities" or "persons specially challenged." The negative or pejorative meanings associated with the older words reflect a long history of "condescension, suspicion and exclusion."

> Trent, J. (1995). *Inventing the feeble mind: A history of mental retardation in the United States*. Berkeley: University of California Press.

People with disabilities "resent words that suggest they're sick, pitiful, childlike, dependent, or objects of admiration. They deplore any image that turns them into poster children, smiling through pain with fund-raising palms out. The word 'invalid' is disliked; so is the phrase 'afflicted with.' Words like 'brave' or 'courageous' are not always appreciated…. They don't like … 'the vertically challenged,' the 'differently abled,' the 'handi-capable,' or the 'physically and mentally challenged.'"

> Mitgang, H. (1993, June 2). Books of the times; the disabled come out fighting. *New York Times*.

WHY THE WORDS CHANGE

A theory is recounted by William Raspberry of the Washington Post. He interviewed Evan Kemp, a leader in disability rights. Kemp says that the labels that are acceptable for an ostracized group are changed every generation or so until that group is accepted as a legitimate part of the culture. The social logic is the logic of replacing words that through use have taken on a demeaning connotation. "Idiot" was replaced by "exceptional." "Crippled" has given way to "handicapped," giving way to "disabled." Ostracized minority groups will continue to insist on a new name as long as they do not feel they are being treated as equals. Government officials have lost their jobs for using the "wrong word" in public. A Secretary of the Interior, James Watt, used the word "cripple" that "tagged him as insensitive and cost him his job." Controlling naming, and wiping away the slur implicit in a current name, is a way for the minority to feel some power.

Raspberry, William (1983, November 14). Names that hurt. *The Washington Post*, pp. A17. Thanks to Phil Calkins for the reference.

THE CONTROVERSY IS NOT SETTLED

"In the United States, a controversy has raged over preferred linguistic usage. One group historically advocated people-first language, expressed in the term 'people with disabilities,' emphasizing the historical roots of American exceptionalism, the importance of the individual in society, and disability as being something not inherent in the person. An equally vocal group has more recently denounced people-first language as offensive, claiming that it was promoted by powerful nondisabled people, particularly advocates for persons with developmental disabilities. This second group prefers the term disabled people, emphasizing minority group identity politics."

"In the United Kingdom, the choice is the term disabled people, signifying in some instances the importance of community and group identity and oppression experiences in the social environment."

Albrecht, G.D., Seelman, K.D., & Bury, M. (2001). The formation of Disability Studies. In G. Albrecht, K. Seelman & M. Bury (Eds.), *Handbook of Disability Studies* (pp. 1-7). Thousand Oaks, CA: Sage.

A CONFUSION OF LABELS

"There is no neutral language with which to discuss disability."

What are the current contexts in which definitions are used? There are many approaches and purposes. "The result is conflict, contradiction, and confusion." "The lack of consistency is most dramatic when a person is defined as disabled in one context and not in another, such that she or he receives therapies for serious impairments but does not qualify for certain disability-related benefits provided by his or her employer or by the government."

Legal and administrative definitions specify who will receive benefits provided by law, or who is subject to civil rights protection. A person who has worked and paid into the Social Security system must demonstrate an inability to engage in gainful employment in order to receive benefits. The definitions under the Americans With Disabilities Act are broader and are constantly challenged and reinterpreted. For example, people whose conditions can be ameliorated by medicine or appliances (for example, hypertension or vision loss) are no longer protected.

Surveys of national populations have the goal of predicting the size and nature of the population with disabilities and have arrived at measures such as the "disability-adjusted life years."

Clinical definitions have their basis in medical authority and pathology, and are used to qualify a patient for rehabilitation, education, or welfare.

Terminology in definitions may be consistent but carry different meanings. Terms include "pathology," "impairment,""functional limitations," and "disability."

An example of applying the new thinking, called the social model:

> "Jim has a condition (pathology) that has resulted in impairments in his musculature that has created a set of functional limitations (restricted use of his arms and legs; inability to walk, lift, finger, or grasp). This has resulted in adaptations to his social performance of things such as self-care behavior and work behavior. He directs his personal assistant in how to do most of his self-care, rather than doing it himself, and he directs his job coach in moving items off shelves and ringing up charges for the customers he assists in the sales job he holds."
>
> Altman, B. (2001). Disability definitions, models, classification schemes, and applications. In G. Albrecht, K. Seelman & M. Bury (Eds.), *Handbook of Disability Studies* (pp. 97-122). Thousand Oaks, CA: Sage.

What is a Disability? Who is Disabled?

"The definition of disability ... is actually one of the most difficult and controversial topics in Disability Studies." -M. Sherry

HIGHLIGHTS

- Physicians have been the gate keepers in defining who has a disability and who is eligible for public assistance and services.
- Medical and related professionals and teachers establish a child's eligibility for special education.
- Physicians also establish eligibility for government services and benefits such as Supplementary Security Income (SSI) and Social Security Disability Insurance (SSDI) and vocational rehabilitation. States have different rules for eligibility.

A CHANGING DEFINITION

The definitions of disability have changed in the last 30 years. In the 1970s, a mental or physical condition was the basis for considering a person disabled. The condition was medically assessed. Now "disability" refers to both the mental or physical condition of the person *and* the ability of the person to function in a physical or technological environment. The new criterion is harder to assess objectively and consistently. It makes it more difficult to measure the incidence of disability via a survey.

> U.S.Census Bureau (2010). Overview.
> http://www.census.gov/hhes/www/disability/overview.html

The definition of disability is contextual and socially constructed. "Whether a particular physical condition is disabling changes with time and place, depending on such factors as social expectations, the state of technology and its availability to people in that condition, the educational system, architecture, attitudes towards physical appearance, and the pace of life."

> Wendell, S. (2010). Toward a feminist theory of disability. In L.J. Davis (Ed.), *The Disability Studies reader* (3rd Ed.) (pp. 336-352). New York: Routledge.

"Disability refers to those *personal, cognitive, physical*, and *behavioral* conditions that have been identified as significantly limiting an individual's ability to function effectively in normal societal situations: family, neighborhood, school, and workplace."

> Osgood, R. L. (2008). *The history of special education: A struggle for equality in American public schools*. Westport, Conn: Praeger.

"Disability exists as it is situated within the larger social context, while impairment is a biological condition."

> Braddock, D. & Parish, S. (2001). An institutional history of disability. In G. Albrecht, K. Seelman & M. Bury (Eds.), *Handbook of Disability Studies* (pp. 11-68). Thousand Oaks, CA: Sage.

CATEGORIES IN EDUCATION

In the United States, a simpler classification is used to decide whether children in public schools are eligible for special education programs. It is codified in the law, The Individuals with Disabilities Education Improvement Act of 2004, and maintained by the U.S. Department of Education. The categories are:

- Specific Learning Disabilities(disorders in psychological processes involved in using language)
- Speech or Language Impairments
- Intellectual Disabilities (deficits in cognitive functioning and adaptive behavior such as mental retardation)
- Emotional Disturbance
- Multiple Disabilities (other issues in combination, impeding learning)
- Hearing Impairments
- Orthopedic Impairments (mobility)
- Other Health Impairments (usually chronic conditions; includes Attention Deficit/Hyperactivity Disorder)
- Autism
- Visual Impairments
- Traumatic Brain Injury (after birth)
- Deaf-Blindness
- Non-Categorical and Developmental Delay (children 3-9 years)

Each category corresponds to guidelines for assessment of children, and appropriate educational strategies and assistive technologies.

> Texas Council for Developmental Disabilities, Project IDEAL. *Disability categories*. Downloaded from http://www.projectidealonline.org/overview.php on May 17, 2010

DIFFERENT PURPOSES

The diagnosis for eligibility for special education is focused on educational needs and may not coincide with the conclusions of a diagnosis by medical or mental health professionals.

> Price, Anne (2010). *Special education disability categories*. BellaOnline. Downloaded from

> http://bellaonline.com/articles/art35159.asp on May 25, 2010. Has good explanations for each category.

"Disability" as an administrative classification is not static. Labeling a person as having a disability implies rights and eligibility for special services. Historically, definitions and classification express various interests and political dynamics.

> Cf. Stone, Deborah (1984). *The disabled state*. Philadelphia: Temple University Press.
> (quoted in Whyte, S.R. & Ingstad, B. (1995). Disability and culture: An overview. In B. Ingstad & S.R. Whyte (Eds.), Disability and culture (pp. 3-34). Berkeley: University of California Press

Early steps to establish a general category of "disabled people" are seen in the census conducted by the British in African colonies, for example, in Tanzania, in 1983. They inventoried people who were chronically unable to work.

> Whyte, S.R. & Ingstad, B. (1995). Disability and culture: An overview. In B. Ingstad & S.R. Whyte (Eds.), *Disability and culture* (pp. 3-34). Berkeley: University of California Press.

The Americans With Disabilities Act defines an individual with a disability as:

1. Having a physical or mental impairment that substantially limits one or more major life activities (e.g., hearing, seeing, speaking, sitting, standing, walking, concentrating, or performing manual tasks)
2. Having a record of such an impairment (in the past, e.g., prior to rehabilitation)
3. Regarded or treated by an employer as having a substantially limiting impairment

> U.S. Equal Employment Opportunity Commission (2008). *Veterans with service-connected disabilities in the workplace and the Americans With Disabilities Act (ADA)*. Downloaded on August 2, 2010 from http://www.eeoc.gov/facts/veterans-disabilities.html

There is an international standard to describe and measure health and disability. It is called the International Classification of Functioning, Disability and Health (abbreviated as ICF). It was maintained in an earlier form since 1980 by the World Health Organization. The current form was ratified in 2001. The ICF offers a way to describe an individual's disability in terms of interaction with the world, regardless of cause: how well can they perform functions needed in "normal" daily life and work? It is designed to be relevant across cultures and age groups. However, application of the label depends on cultural norms.

The ICF has two lists: a list of body functions and structure, and a list of domains of activity and participation. For example, among body functions, there are: mental, sensory and pain, voice and speech, neuromuscular, and so on. Body structures refer to parts of the anatomy. Among activities are: learning and applying knowledge, general tasks, communication, mobility, self-care, and so on.

The ICF represents a shift in thinking about disability. Instead of seeing disability as a medical or biological condition, it focuses on the ability to function and participate in society. It is based on the notion that everyone can suffer a disability at some time, and that disability is a universal experience.

The ICF makes it possible for countries to survey their populations and report characteristics in a uniform way internationally. It may be too complex for everyday uses, but it provides a standard framework for global communication about health and disability.

> *Classification of diseases, functioning, and disability*. Centers for Disease Control and Prevention, National Center for Health Statistics. Downloaded from http://www.cdc.gov/nchs/icd/icf.htm on May 26, 2010.
>
> For example classifications, see an online version of the ICF at http://apps.who.int/classifications/icfbrowser/
>
> World Health Organization, Collaborating Center for the Classification of Diseases (1993-). International classification of impairments, disabilities, and handicaps. Geneva: WHO. Reprinted annually.

The ICF represents a movement to the social model of impairment, and away from the medical model. It recognizes that disability is a complex phenomenon that requires multiple levels of analysis including medical and socio-political. It also recognizes that disability is not a minority issue, but one that affects an entire society.

> Shakespeare, T. (2010). The social model of disability. In L.J. Davis (Ed.), *The Disability Studies reader* (3rd Ed.) (pp. 266-273). New York: Routledge.

KEY FOR ACCESS TO SERVICES

"In Europe and North America, disability is a political privilege entitling one to financial support and a series of services. The state assigns to physicians the task of determining who is entitled to these rights. In this way, the political issue of redistribution, which involves separating the deserving from the undeserving, becomes a clinical problem."

> Whyte, S.R. & Ingstad, B. (1995). Disability and culture: An overview. In B. Ingstad & S.R. Whyte (Eds.), *Disability and culture* (pp. 3-34). Berkeley: University of California Press.

"Disability as a formal administrative category is designed to differentiate between those who must work and those who are morally entitled to public benefits." There was concern about malingering and abuse – laggards. Having doctors act as the gatekeepers was to ensure objective medical standards and consistency.

> Scotch, Richard K. (2001). American disability policy in the 20th Century. In P.K. Longmore & L. Umansky (Eds.) *The new disability history: American perspectives* (pp. 375-392). New York: New York University Press.

"No one wants the social stigma associated with disability, but social recognition of disability determines the practical help a person receives from doctors, government agencies, insurance companies, charity organizations, and often from family and friends. Thus, how a society defines disability and whom it recognizes as disabled are of enormous psychological, economic and social importance."

> Wendell, S. (2010). Toward a feminist theory of disability. In L.J. Davis (Ed.), *The Disability Studies reader* (3rd Ed.) (pp. 336-352). New York: Routledge.

DISABILITY AS IDENTITY

We can speak of "disabilities" as impairments, and "disabling barriers" as things in the environment that limit the rights and freedoms of people with disabilities.

"The definition of disability … is actually one of the most difficult and controversial topics in Disability Studies."

An alternative to the definition of disability in the social model is the one popular in the U.S., which is "to approach disability as an identity, and to regard people with disabilities as a minority group." "There is a debate over who is 'really disabled' – who has an 'authentic' disability identity."

The question is who names who… "I generally do not use 'people-first language' because I want to emphasize the political nature of choices made by people around identity."

"Disability occurs alongside multiple other identities (such as sexuality, 'race' and ethnicity, socioeconomic status, etc). "Identity politics around disability has tended to downplay, ignore, or underestimate the diversity of people who may be identified as 'disabled.'"

"Disability Studies has only just begun to analyze the ways in which disability and other forms of inequality are implicated in certain forms of power, normativity, and marginalization." We need to shift away from the ways in which disabled people are a minority group and instead focus on ways in which certain bodies are constructed in medical, legal, social, educational, and economic discourse."

Sherry, M. (2008). *Disability and Diversity: A Sociological Perspective*. New York: Nova Science Publishers.

NOT A HOMOGENEOUS GROUP

The phrase "persons with disabilities" encompasses many subgroups with significantly different circumstances. For example, older people may become disabled by virtue of aging and declining health. There are young people with severe cognitive disabilities who will probably never learn enough to navigate daily activities, let alone a job. In between, however, are many persons with disabilities who were until recently abandoned and excluded from community and work who with help are able to participate.

Obviously, some disabilities are *visible* to others (for example, motor skills, the ability to see or hear), and some are *invisible* (for example, learning disabilities). Disabilities can be the result of an accident, inherited genes, or an illness. Some people are born disabled, and some people become disabled. People who reach an advanced age may experience a disability, but usually long after they need to go to school, tend to families, or earn a living. A disability can be temporary, because the illness or condition causing it is cured, for example, a blind person regains sight.

The implications for social acceptance, for potential assistance, and ultimately for participation in community and work in our current society can be vastly different.

The historical and research summaries below show that various subgroups have had different circumstances and opportunities.

Research, educational interventions, special education, and assistive technology have made dramatic differences for a wide range of people with disabilities, but not all of them equally.

How Many People Have Disabilities?

"Fewer than 15% of disabilities are present from birth; the other 85% are acquired." - N.B. Miller and C.C. Sammons.

HOW MANY?

- *One in ten* adults of working age has a disability. (It is one in five if you include the whole population.)
- Among adults of working age, the most prevalent disability is "difficulty walking or using stairs" (5.2%), followed by a cognitive disability (4.2%), hearing disability (2.1%). About 1.8% have difficulty dressing or bathing, and 3.5% have difficulty running errands.
- Roughly 15% of persons with disabilities were *born* with their disability. 85% were disabled *after birth*, due to illness, accidents, war and other causes.
- About 35% of persons with disabilities of working age are employed. This is less than half the rate of employment for able-bodied people (74%).

INTERNATIONAL PREVALENCE

"The first estimates by the World Health Organization [in 1980?] were that 10 percent of any population was disabled. Later these figures were modified to **6 or 7 percent**." Obviously, there were different definitions of what was included, the severity required to label something "disabling," and how data was gathered.

Whyte, S.R. & Ingstad, B. (1995). Disability and culture: An overview. In B. Ingstad & S.R. Whyte (Eds.), *Disability and culture* (pp. 3-34). Berkeley: University of California Press.

RELATED TO POVERTY

Worldwide, a rough estimate is that "one in ten persons lives with a cognitive or physical disability, and according to UN estimates, 80 percent live in developing countries." Up to 50 percent of the people in the poorest countries do not have access to modern health care, sanitation facilities, or safe drinking water.

Davidson, M. (2010). Universal design: The work of disability in the age of globalization. In L.J. Davis (Ed.), *The Disability Studies reader* (3rd Ed.) (pp. 133-146). New York: Routledge.

U.S. POPULATION

The statistics below are derived from data in the American Community Survey of 2009, U.S. Census Bureau.

The prevalence of disability among people living in the community (as opposed to institutions such as prisons, hospitals and such) is 12.0% across all ages. By age group:

- 0.7% of children younger than 5 years old
- 5.2 of children 5-17 years old
- **10.1 of adults of working age, 18 to 64 years old**
- 37.4 of adults over 65

By Type of Disability

Within the U.S. population of **working age (18 to 64 years old)**, by types of disabilities:

- 2.1% have a hearing disability
- 1.7 have a vision disability
- 4.2 have a cognitive disability
- 5.2 have an ambulatory disability (serious difficulty walking or climbing stairs)
- 1.8 have a "self-care" disability (difficulty dressing or bathing)
- 3.5 have difficulty with "independent living" (difficulty running errands)

Employment

The rate of employment within the U.S. population of **working age (18 to 64 years old)**:

- 35.3% of those with disabilities are employed
- 74.3% of those without disabilities are employed

The rate of employment varies by disability:

- 51.6% of those with hearing disabilities are employed
- 38.3% of those with vision disabilities are employed
- 24.4% of those with cognitive disabilities are employed
- 26.2% of those with ambulatory disabilities are employed

When the definition of "employed" means working full time, year round, the numbers are lower, but there is still a large gap:

20.4% of those with disabilities are employed full time, year round
50.8% of those without disabilities are employed full time, year round

Rate of Poverty

Within the U.S. population of **working age (18 to 64 years old)**, the rate of poverty for those with disabilities is nearly double, overall:

26.4% of those with disabilities are living in poverty
11.7% of those without disabilities are living in poverty

Veterans

Among civilian veterans over 18 years old, 25.6% have a disability.

Poverty rates among civilian veterans of working age (18 to 64 years old) are:

15.8% of civilian veterans with a disability live in poverty
 6.0% of civilian veterans without a disability live in poverty

> Rehabilitation Research and Training Center on Disability Statistics and Demographics (2010). *Annual disability statistics compendium 2010*. Downloaded from http://www.neweditions.net/statsrrtc/compendium2010.pdf. Source of data is the U.S. Census Bureau, American Community Survey, 2009. The data cited above is from multiple tables, 1.3 through 6.3.

OBSERVATIONS

These generalizations are slightly dated (1999) but could hold true:

- "Fewer than 15% of disabilities are present from birth; the other 85% are acquired."
- Many people become impaired due to accidents (car, sports, gunshot), or illness, e.g., strokes, arthritis, and asthma
- Among non-visible impairments are diabetes, heart disease, lupus, asthma, depression, chronic fatigue syndrome, and epilepsy
- "One in four families has a member with mental illness."
- "Nearly one in five children has a reading disability."

- "Mental retardation affects 100 times as many people as total blindness does."

> Miller, N. B. & Sammons, C.C. (1999). *Everybody's Different: Understanding and Changing Our Reactions to Disabilities*. Baltimore: Paul H. Brookes Pub. Co.

RATE OF EMPLOYMENT COMPARED INTERNATIONALLY

The rate of employment for persons with disabilities is 58% in the United States (2002). This compares with 72% in France and 79% in Switzerland. The U.S. ranks #12 internationally on this indicator.

(Calculated as the employment rate of disabled persons as a percentage of non-disabled persons 20 to 64 years old, late 1990s.)

> Annex to GECD Society at a Glance 2002. , Table SS5.1 Downloaded from http://www.nationmaster.com/graph/peo_dis_per_emp-people-disabled-persons-employment

THOSE LIVING IN "GROUP QUARTERS"

The statistics shown above from the U.S. Census *exclude* a count of people with disabilities living in institutional settings. People living in group quarters such as correctional facilities, nursing facilities, in-patient hospices, residential schools, and hospitals are subject to a separate survey because their needs are addressed by their facilities and not through public services.

There are different characteristics, of course, pertaining to people living in group quarters (called GQ's). **The disability rate here (2008) is 49.4 percent**, for example. In adult correctional facilities, the rate is 28.8 percent. In nursing facilities, it is 97.3 percent. Most of the population living in group quarters are in prison (39.6%). The next largest group is in nursing facilities (35.4%). More than half of those living in group quarters are between the ages of 15 and 24.

> Brault, Matthew (2008). *Disability status and the characteristics or people in group quarters: a brief analysis of disability prevalence among the civilian non-institutionalized and total populations in the American Community Survey*. Washington, DC: U.S. Census Bureau.

AUTISM AND TRAUMATIC BRAIN INJURY

"The most accepted prevalence rate for autism is 10 per 10,000 (.1%), a rate derived from analysis of 32 separate prevalence surveys conducted between 1966 and 2001. This rate is highly contested however. Some autism advocates and professionals who work with this population claim an incidence rate of approximately 1 in 150 (.67%). Without question, the prevalence rate has been steadily rising in the past decade, but whether this is due to improved diagnostic procedures or an actual increase in incidence is unclear."

"About 80,000 to 90,000 of the 475,000 children who have sustained traumatic brain injuries (TBIs) are permanently disabled from their accidents or injuries. About 180 per 100,000 children under age 15 experience TBIs and of that number, 5% to 8% experience severe TBIs."

> Texas Council for Developmental Disabilities, Project IDEAL (2009). *Disability categories*. Downloaded on May 17, 2010 from http://www.projectidealonline.org/overview.php

IQ

Mental retardation (IDEA category) is an IQ of 69 or below. General estimates are that about 2% of the population is in this IQ range.

> Price, Anne (2010). *Special education disability categories*. BellaOnline. Downloaded from http://bellaonline.com/articles/art35159.asp on May 25, 2010. Has good explanations for each category.

Historical Timeline

"People with disabilities have shared a history that has often been oppressive and included abuse, neglect, sterilization, stigma, euthanasia, segregation, and institutionalization."

-D. Braddock & S. Parish

The following section is a series of snapshots from various sources. The main purpose is to tell the story of society's struggle with the fact that some people are going to be disabled. The worst treatments, historically, were usually responses to extreme impairments, especially intellectual impairment and extreme deformation, especially in children. We have to remember that the definition, or social construction, of disability keeps changing. There are times when persons with disabilities, the poor, and the criminal were equated. Also times when immigrants with asthma were rejected for their impairment.

IN SUMMARY

"Persons with significant and obvious disabling conditions have been demonized, deified, ignored, persecuted, protected, or isolated and exterminated."

> Osgood, R. L. (2008). *The history of special education: A struggle for equality in American public schools.* Westport, Conn: Praeger.

The best source for history is the paper by Braddock and Parish, which is cited often below.

> Braddock, D. & Parish, S. (2001). An institutional history of disability. In G. Albrecht, K. Seelman & M. Bury (Eds.), *Handbook of Disability Studies* (pp. 11-68). Thousand Oaks, CA: Sage.

An excellent, light and colorful history mainly in the form of photographs is available online.

> State of Alaska, Governor's Council on Disabilities and Special Education (2010). *Disability history exhibit*. Downloaded November 2, 2010 from http://www.hss.state.ak.us/gcdse/history/

A different set of details in a style lighter than a formal history are available online, from a community-generated social history project.

> Disability Social History Project
> http://www.disabilityhistory.org/timeline_new.html

ANCIENT TIMES

Keywords for this era: punishment from God or gods, some infanticide, slavery

The Old Testament recognizes a charitable obligation to people with disabilities, while it is also sees impairments as a punishment from God.

Notions of impairment in Greece and Rome accepted the belief that persons with congenital impairments embodied the wrath/anger of the gods and should be killed. Yet this view coexisted with the fact that those who acquired their disabilities later in life were often integrated into society as workers, citizens, and soldiers.

Life expectancy in ancient Greece and Rome did not exceed 37 years for women and 44 years for men. Infanticide was not as widespread as has been believed. In Sparta, children with physical impairments were put to death. In Greece & Rome, infanticide was done mainly for economic reasons. There was public support for men disabled by war, and military medicine was in widespread use.

During the Roman Empire, short slaves and slaves with intellectual disabilities were kept by wealthy men for entertainment. It was considered good luck to have them. Court jesters are seen among Egyptian pharaohs, in China, and in pre-Colombian America.

<blockquote>Braddock, D. & Parish, S. (2001). An institutional history of disability. In G. Albrecht, K. Seelman & M. Bury (Eds.), Handbook of Disability Studies (pp. 11-68). Thousand Oaks, CA: Sage.</blockquote>

ANCIENT ROOTS, BIAS

What are the roots of discrimination against disabled people? Are they rooted in a "natural" fear of the unknown and the unfamiliar? There is evidence of bias in the earliest cultures of Western civilization.

The Old Testament (Leviticus) says that religious rituals may not be performed by people with certain imperfections. The Roman Catholic Church until recently prohibited people with learning difficulties from receiving some sacraments.

The ancient Greeks and Romans "placed a high priority on the care of those injured and subsequently disabled in battle" but "they were enthusiastic advocates of infanticide for sickly or deformed children."

In the Middle Ages, disabled people "were the subject of superstition, persecution and rejection." Disability was associated with evil and witchcraft. "Deformed and disabled children were seen as 'changelings' or the Devil's substitutes for human children." There was the idea that physical or mental impairment was punishment for wrongdoing. Martin Luther "saw the Devil" in disabled children and recommended killing them. Shakespeare created Richard III as a man twisted in both body and mind, and reviled for his deformity, making him seek revenge as a villain. Joke books in Tudor and Stuart England make fun and ridicule disabled people. "Idiots" were objects of entertainment.

<blockquote>Barnes, Colin (2010). A brief history of discrimination and disabled people. In L.J. Davis (Ed.), The Disability Studies reader (3rd Ed.) (pp. 20-32). New York: Routledge.</blockquote>

MIDDLE AGES

Keywords: Christian charity, hospices, supernatural or satanic causes

During the Middle Ages, there was a widespread belief that demons caused impairments. At the same time, there were religious movements preaching compassion and support toward persons with disabilities. Development of the first residential institutions for persons with disabilities is traced to the Middle Ages.

During the 4th to 6th Centuries, monasteries had hospices for blind and intellectually disabled people. Many conditions thought to have supernatural or demonological causes, for example, the Devil caused epilepsy. Mental illness could be cured by exorcism.

However, medical texts saw natural causes behind impairments. As much as 75% of population was poor and suffered malnutrition and disease at the time. Many were not capable of working. There was a rise in begging. There was no stigma in begging

There was a distinction between "fools and idiots" – those with intellectual disabilities, and "lunatics"—those with mental illnesses. The English Crown in 13th Century could take custody of the property of idiots, but not lunatics. Lunatics were protected, and they did not lose their property.

> Braddock, D. & Parish, S. (2001). An institutional history of disability. In G. Albrecht, K. Seelman & M. Bury (Eds.), *Handbook of Disability Studies* (pp. 11-68). Thousand Oaks, CA: Sage.

"In the Middle Ages, impairments were not specifically distinguished from other forms of misery or suffering. Infirmity and poverty were part of God's varied creation—the order of things. The response to difference was charity, spirituality, and morality…. The infirm were marginal, cared for by their families or by charitable patrons." Poor and disabled people were equally objects of charity.

> Whyte, Susan Reynolds (1995). Disability between discourse and experience. In B. Ingstad & S.R. Whyte (Eds.), *Disability and culture* (pp. 267-291). Berkeley: University of California Press.

RENAISSANCE 14th-16th CENTURIES

Keywords: alms houses, mad houses and prisons; primitive medical cures; sign language invented

Early medicine shows studies of anatomy and physiology related to hearing, vision, and the body. Witch hunts were discouraged, although there was a belief that people with mental disabilities had a bestial nature and were possessed by Satan. Treatments could include beating the head, or boring holes in the head to release "black bile."

In England, there was a distinction made between "safe" versus "dangerous" people with mental disabilities. A statute of 1388 in England distinguished between the "deserving" and the "un-deserving" poor. People with disabilities were "deserving." Poor criminals were "undeserving."

In the 16th century, we see the education of deaf people. Aristocratic children are taught in monasteries and convents. Sign language was developed in the Turkish Ottoman court around 1500. "Mutes" were used as attendants because they could not hear court secrets. Their signing became well known.

Disabled people (and the sick, elderly, and poor) who were rejected by their families depended on alms and begging for subsistence up to the 17th Century. The Christian Church provided charity and maintained small medieval hospitals for the severely impaired.

The Poor Law of 1601 in England marks an official recognition that disabled people need state assistance. This came about as the Christian Church lost its ability to maintain hospitals, and "bands of beggars" demanded help.

During the 13-17th Centuries, poverty in general was deemed suspect. The poor were incarcerated, along with the mentally ill. Begging was outlawed.

> Barnes, Colin (2010). A brief history of discrimination and disabled people. In L.J. Davis (Ed.), *The Disability Studies reader* (3rd Ed.) (pp. 20-32). New York: Routledge.

17th CENTURY

Keywords: scientific approach; shift to community support; government institutions for people with disabilities

During the Age of Reason and Enlightenment, we find John Locke distinguishing between idiots and madmen in an essay.

Francis Bacon (1605) argued for the collection of empirical data and experiments – a scientific approach. He refuted the notion that divine punishment was the cause of mental illness.

A model begun in England migrated to early America: local communities were charged with providing for persons in need. This was a shift from family support. Poverty, disability and the inability to work were seen as interconnected.

First alms house in the U.S. was in Boston in 1662, for various orphans, elderly, poor, deaf, and blind. Madhouses spread through England at this time.

Infirmity began to be viewed in medical terms. The concern was less to explain why infirmities exist, and more to make an inventory of impairments.

In the 17th Century, there began the idea of confinement of the infirm in hospitals. Institutions arose specifically for the care of disabled people, especially soldiers and seamen, and for the mentally ill.

18th CENTURY

Keywords: special education; schools for blind and deaf children; idea of rehabilitation and treatment; madhouse and prison confinement

The idea of improving the lives of disabled people through education is a phenomenon of 18th Century Enlightenment. Schools for blind and deaf children were founded.

> Whyte, Susan Reynolds (1995). Disability between discourse and experience. In B. Ingstad & S.R. Whyte (Eds.), *Disability and culture* (pp. 267-291). Berkeley: University of California Press.

"...to the cusp of the eighteenth century, disability was strongly influenced by the rise of the scientific method during the Renaissance and by changing public perceptions toward poverty and disability." During the Enlightenment, scientists distinguished mental illness from intellectual disability. ... Physicians, educators, and caretakers ascended in the lives of persons with disabilities. ... Scientific inquiry into medical aspects led to classification schemes.. and resulted in the development of specialized treatments and residential and educational services ... but also established and reinforced notions of the boundaries between normalcy and aberrance."

In the 18th Century, madhouses and criminal prisons were combined. Inmates were expected to work. The wealthy sought private confinement for family members. Idleness and poverty were criminalized. Houses of correction, workhouses, asylums, and madhouses were common.

There was the view that disability was not God's will and that society could intervene and rehabilitate persons with disabilities. There was a rise in experimental treatments.

"In the American colonies, persons with impairments were often perceived to menace the economic well-being of the community." Since towns were responsible for the "underclass," they discouraged beggars and idle people, "warning them" out of town.

1752 saw the first general hospital, introduced by Thomas Bond and Benjamin Franklin, for persons with mental disabilities.

18th century saw the proliferation of residential schools for deaf and blind children.

Veterans of the Revolutionary War were the first people with disabilities in the U.S. to receive a pension, as compensation for war-related impairments.

Kentucky was one of first to establish payment to families for the care of mentally ill or intellectually disabled family members. They used a trial system for determining "idiots" versus "lunatics."

"In the colonial and early national eras of the United States, persons with disabilities either were kept at home, tolerated and even supported by communities, or expelled, prosecuted, and even condemned. Before the early nineteenth century, deaf and blind people, the physically crippled, and those with various vaguely defined yet obvious forms of mental incapacity constituted the visible and thus recognized population, of persons with disabilities. Public policies such as 'warning out' (a method of excluding nonresident poor from local communities), institutions such as the colonial mental hospital in Williamsburg, VA, and private efforts of persons such as Thomas Gallaudet and Samuel Gridley Howe represented different approaches."

Osgood, R. L. (2008). The history of special education: A struggle for equality in American public schools. Westport, Conn: Praeger.

19th CENTURY

Keywords: specialized residential institutions (hospitals, asylums, workhouses, prisons); segregation from community; state control; freak shows; segregating children in school; interest in treatment and cure

"The Asylum for the Deaf in Hartford, CT, opened in 1817. Asylum for the Blind and another for Idiotic and Feebleminded Youth opened in Massachusetts in 1832 and 1848. Interest in institutionalizing, educating, treating, and even curing persons with disabilities thus grew steadily as the century progressed."

"The perceived need for greater control over individuals and social groups—especially of poor and/or immigrant populations—grew. …Thus by 1900, disability had become a key construct and target for progressive reformers."

Osgood, R. L. (2008). *The history of special education: A struggle for equality in American public schools*. Westport, Conn: Praeger.

The numbers of hospitals, asylums, workhouses and prisons increased. These represent the segregation of disabled people into residential institutions. One of the causes for this trend was large-scale urban industrialization. Urban factories displaced cottage industries and agriculture as sources of work. Poverty spread, especially in rural communities. Factory work was regimented and demanded able-bodied workers and physical fitness.

A state-run system of institutions was created in England, in 1845, due to charges by reformers that private asylums had atrocious conditions and were cruel.

In England, reforms introduced uniformity in the national welfare system, denial of help outside of institutions, and deterrence as a basis for support. Deterrence was meant to make malingerers miserable. The policies expressed a mistrust of people claiming charity. The Poor Laws separated people consigned to workhouses into groups: able-bodied males, able-bodied females, children, and the aged and infirm. The groups were housed separately. People who were both disabled and poor were further divided into "sick," "insane," "defective," and "aged and infirm."

The "insane" were either admitted to an asylum or boarded out to caretaking families. They were "idiots," "lunatics," "mad," "mentally infirm," or "suffering diseases of the brain."

Lunacy Legislation in England in 1845 required doctors to certify mental illness. After the 1871 Poor Law in England, officials could commit the insane against their will. "Hence, 1845 can be seen as the start of the medical profession's subsequent domination of all aspects of disability."

An upsurge of Christian values led to the decline of the practice of infanticide for disabled children.

"Defectives" included people who were blind, deaf, mute, epileptic, and "mentally subnormal." Charities specializing in these groups arose, especially for blind and deaf people.

In the 19th century, primitive, exotic, and deformed people were put on display in museums, circuses, fairs, and freak shows. They included bearded ladies, "pin heads," Siamese twins, people missing limbs, dwarfs, and giants. One of the well-known examples was Joseph Merrick, the Elephant Man. He was lifted out of a freak show by a doctor. Gradually there was the feeling that "freaks belong in medical textbooks and not in sideshows." Freak shows were shut down as indecent and exploitative of suffering individuals. Notably, like Merrick who was mute, impaired people were still objectified – first as freaks and then as objects of charity.

At the same time as large public school systems developed, attitudes and beliefs regarding disability became more negative, and disabled children were differentiated into more specialized categories. The number of children identified as disabled grew. Public schools took on the task of identifying, segregating, instructing, and controlling children whose disabilities were seen as difficult, dangerous, or untreatable.

When Boston established "intermediate schools" or "schools for special instruction," their purpose was to isolate temporarily older, non-English-speaking immigrant children. However, soon other children who disrupted standard classes were removed to these schools. Boston school officials learned that as public elementary and secondary schools grew in size and became more crowded, stratified, and regimented, it became necessary to provide alternative placements for children who were seriously struggling intellectually, physically, or behaviorally. Other cities created settings for the incorrigible, unruly, struggling, and imbecile. Some became more schools for truants. Life in these schools was difficult for both students and teachers. Teachers assigned to them were lower achievers themselves, and not trained for the special populations. Non-English-speaking children struggled to learn language and assimilate, lending to the public belief that they were intellectually deficient and obstinate. The terms "ungraded" and "special" were used synonymously. In Boston and other cities, the majority of students were male.

There were debates among educators whether it was better to segregate or institutionalize the feebleminded. They were a burden to teachers, and made little progress in normal classrooms. The prevailing view was to keep children with disabilities in the public schools. The motivations for creating special education were several: to better educate "normal" children and disabled children, to control certain elements of the student population, and, to improve the efficiency of school systems. They served to help assimilate diverse ethnic groups.

> Barnes, Colin (2010). A brief history of discrimination and disabled people. In L.J. Davis (Ed.), *The Disability Studies reader* (3rd Ed.) (pp. 20-32). New York: Routledge.

In non-industrial societies, people with disabilities typically live with their family and within local communities. The industrial revolution disrupted families as people moved into urban areas for employment. The care of people with disabilities shifted to local government. This resulted in the rise of the "asylum movement." People with disabilities were moved into institutions. Some were supported by private religious or charitable groups also. Some institutions offered education and rehabilitation, and others were primarily custodial.

> Scotch, Richard K. (2001). American disability policy in the 20th Century. In P.K. Longmore & L. Umansky (Eds.) *The new disability history: American perspectives* (pp. 375-392). New York: New York University Press.

In the 19th Century, there were more residential schools for deaf and blind people. For example, in 1817, Thomas Gallaudet and Laurent Clerc founded the American Asylum for the Education of the Deaf and Dumb in Harford CT. Within 2 years, 11 states were sending students.

The education of deaf people became controversial, with a split between the "oralists" who thought deaf people should learn to read lips and speak, and "manualists" who thought sign language was the answer to communication. (See more on this in a section below.)

Later in 1864, Gallaudet University was founded by Alexander Graham Bell. He urged that we banish the use of sign language and encourage people who were deaf to "pass" as hearing. In 1880, the National Association of the Deaf was organized by deaf people, to fight the oralists.

There were those who saw deaf people who used sign language as "less evolved," "like apes or racial minorities." This view led to eradication of manual education. "Sign language survived and thrived during nearly a century of repression, and it is now a primary communication strategy in educating deaf children."

Louis Braille invented a tactile writing system for blind readers in 1824. (Standard Braille came later, in 1932.)

People with mental illness and intellectual disability were segregated from society. The first mental hospital appeared in Mexico City in 1566. The first American almshouse appeared in 1662. The first mental asylum appeared in Virginia in 1773. There was a significant rise of institutions after 1820s in America. Historians do not agree on why this happened. Was it social upheaval, an effort to manage and control deviant members of society?

After the 1840s, there were more mental asylums. Dorothea Dix advocated to construct humane residences for the insane. Initially, middle class and poor inmates were separated. The asylums were overcrowded almost immediately. Caretakers sought to release residents into the community. They provided ever less education and "moral treatment," and more care-taking.

With the rise of institutions, there was a rise of professional caretakers whose livelihood depended on the institutional system. Psychiatric power had grown in the 17th & 18th Centuries, as did the trend toward involuntary institutionalization. (It persists today.) Between 1850-1890, 55 state psychiatric institutions were built, holding about 41,000 people. By 1910, they held 188,000 people.

Overcrowding led to a retreat to family care. After the Civil War, there was a period of general economic hardship and institutions could not discharge inmates, so they put them to work. This led to exploitation of residents as labor. A peonage system prevailed. "Training schools" evolved into custodial asylums.

There were abuses: for example, husbands could commit wives to asylums, for disobedience.

The national census counted "idiots" and "insane," deaf and blind people starting in 1830, although the census for this category was not continuous. The count was later shown to mix characteristics of race and insanity; they were implicitly racist.

By the 19th Century there were institutions for "correcting the body" in terms of motor skills. There were dynamic changes in the education of people with disabilities, for example, the provision of speech therapy.

Through the 19th century, there continued to be freak shows at circuses, fairs, and expositions. Subjects were "sold" to organizers.

Between 1880-1925, people with intellectual disabilities came to be viewed as deviant social menaces who were incurable. An intellectual movement called eugenics arose, expressing a fear that the human species was being degraded. Newly invented intelligence tests were used to identify and to segregate children. "Society needed protection and institutions were the answer." At the time, physicians were refusing to treat infants with birth defects.

The oppression of disabled people intensified in the 19th Century due to philosophies emphasizing "egocentric" thinking and Darwinism. Darwin's theory of evolution holds that natural selection rewards optimal adaptation, the fittest survive, and evolution is progress. Darwinism appealed to the rich and successful as a justification for their wealth, status and power. In their view, the suffering of the disadvantaged was the price of progress.

The first rumblings of activism are the political organization of deaf advocates in the 19th Century. At the same time, people with disabilities were exploited in freak shows, and eugenics began.

EARLY 20th CENTURY

Keywords: residential institutions for people with mental disabilities; segregation of children in schools; poor farms; eugenics; sterilization; murder; shock therapy; persons with disabilities speak up

Eugenicists build on fears about the "health" of the human race. They saw genetic links between physical and mental impairments and social evils such as crime and unemployment. They thought sterilization and life-time segregation was a means of protecting the integrity of the race. The fear of mental illness led to mandatory IQ testing in British schools. The idea of compulsory sterilization was considered in England and in the U.S.

> Barnes, Colin (2010). A brief history of discrimination and disabled people. In L.J. Davis (Ed.), *The Disability Studies reader* (3rd Ed.) (pp. 20-32). New York: Routledge.

In the early 20th Century, there was a dramatic expansion of residential institutions for people with mental disabilities, and segregation of children in public schools. However, later in the century we see a massive movement toward de-institutionalization -- toward independent living, the emergence of family, community and consumer advocacy, and litigation that forged a constitutional right to treatment for persons with mental disabilities. Later in the century also, children with disabilities are re-integrated in mainstream schools.

By 1920s, poor farms were dumping grounds for all "undesirables." Most (70 %-85%) of the residents were deemed "feebleminded."

Between 1907 and 1949, some states sterilized residents with intellectual disabilities. There were 47,000 recorded sterilizations in 30 states. In the eyes of caretakers at the time, sterilization made it socially acceptable to release the residents into communities. The Supreme Court affirmed states' rights to sterilize individuals.

"In 1933, using California's program as a model, Nazi Germany enacted its own eugenic sterilization law" which led to forced sterilization of 300,000 to 400,000 in Germany. Later, murder by euthanasia of 200-275,000 between 1939 and 1945 in Germany. Psychiatrists were responsible for identifying victims. Sterilizations were carried out in Denmark and Sweden during the 1930s and 1940s, also.

Secular charitable organizations like the Red Cross became forerunners of vocational rehabilitation. Red Cross established an Institute for Crippled and Disabled Men in 1917 for veterans.

There was a workmen's compensation law in 1902. It was the first legal protection for workers, e.g., men injured in the workplace. There was public concern about rehabilitation and training for disabled workers. Goodwill Industries was established in 1902. It hired unemployed people to repair donated goods, and later, provided sheltered work for persons with disabilities.

Better prosthetics after WWI made it possible for more disabled veterans to work.

> Braddock, D. & Parish, S. (2001). An institutional history of disability. In G. Albrecht, K. Seelman & M. Bury (Eds.), *Handbook of Disability Studies* (pp. 11-68). Thousand Oaks, CA: Sage.

The modern idea of rehabilitation was a byproduct of World War I. Many men survived the war but with wounds and mutilations. Prostheses were developed. The idea arose that all congenital and acquired impairments could be reconstructed, replaced or compensated by devices. Infirmities were seen as technical problems that could be solved, with the goal of re-assimilating the person into society.

> Whyte, Susan Reynolds (1995). Disability between discourse and experience. In B. Ingstad & S.R. Whyte (Eds.), *Disability and culture* (pp. 267-291). Berkeley: University of California Press.

"The development of disability as a concern of the state was accompanied by the emergence of rehabilitation as a medical and paramedical specialization, beginning in the struggle for professional control over the damaged bodies of the First World War. …as federal legislation on disability expanded, and as the health insurance industry developed, disability became big business."

> Gritzer, Glenn & Arluke, Arnold (1985). *The making of rehabilitation: A political economy of medical specialization, 1890-1980*. Berkeley: University of California Press.
>
> Quoted in Whyte, S.R. & Ingstad, B. (1995). Disability and culture: An overview. In B. Ingstad & S.R. Whyte (Eds.), *Disability and culture* (pp. 3-34). Berkeley: University of California Press.

"World War I, with its terrible production of mutilated men, led to a consciousness of disability and a whole set of rehabilitation institutions."

> Whyte, S.R. & Ingstad, B. (1995). Disability and culture: An overview. In B. Ingstad & S.R. Whyte (Eds.), *Disability and culture* (pp. 3-34). Berkeley: University of California Press.

A paternalistic approach – the welfare state—grew for a number of reasons after the 1940s. A big factor was concern for disabled veterans of the two World Wars. In England, legislation finally addressed disabled people as a group, and their right to employment, along with rehabilitation and vocational training services.

> Barnes, Colin (2010). A brief history of discrimination and disabled people. In L.J. Davis (Ed.), *The Disability Studies reader* (3rd Ed.) (pp. 20-32). New York: Routledge.

LATE 20th CENTURY

Keywords: community-based support programs; independent living in communities; disabilities rights movement; biographical writings; laws protecting and supporting persons with disabilities; Federal funding; anti-psychotic drugs; parent advocates

Community-based mental health programs expanded after the creation of the National Institute of Mental Health in 1946.

First biographical writings by blind people pointed to their social and physical environment as the biggest barrier, not their impairment. The social model of disability—the view that society "creates" what we think is a disability-- came out of social constructivism movement in education and social science in the 1960s.

1950s saw the emergence of organizations of parents around intellectual disabilities, e.g., National Association for Retarded Children. They advocated for rights and for services.

Anti-psychotic drugs were invented during the 1950s. This resulted in the release of more patients from psychiatric hospitals into the community, and a trend toward community-based treatment. Residence in psychiatric hospitals went from a high of 559,000 in 1955 to about 359,000 in 1974. Homelessness of people with intellectual disabilities was reduced due to better community services and support.

However, many charged that even up to the 1960s "American society still treated persons with intellectual disabilities as a group that needed to be controlled by segregation, sterilization, and isolation." In 1960 President Kennedy stated a need for a national plan in the field of mental retardation. He formed a President's Panel. He also signed Community Mental Health Centers Act of 1963.

There was a landmark legal case in 1966 which granted rights to a person who was involuntarily committed to a psychiatric hospital, because confinement could not be considered a punishment and therefore the person did not lose their rights.

A 1971 law enabled states to obtain federal funding for institutional services for people with intellectual disabilities if the care met minimal federal standards of treatment and space. They could be reimbursed for 50-78% of costs. States were able to reduce overcrowding. There followed a tidal wave of class action suits about conditions in institutions. This represented a shift in the burden of support from states to the Federal government.

In 1973 there were protests against the delay in implementing the regulations regarding Section 504 of Rehabilitation Act. Television showed first protests, as disabled advocates organized sit-ins in Federal offices. They were finally successfully (regarding implementation) in 1977.

The "Section 504 protests" brought together people across all disabilities, sharing one agenda.

With the Education for All Handicapped Children's Act of 1975, parents had for the first time a federally enforced right to education for children with disabilities. This created a sense of entitlement. By 1996, 46 % of children with disabilities were schooled in regular classroom settings, while the rest were still separate. By 1996, 11% of deaf children and 8% of blind children remained in residential schools. That is, about 90% were in regular school classes.

1970s saw the rise of independent living. The potential for independent living was expressed in the Vocational Rehabilitation Act of 1973 Section 504: "Barriers are less about individual impairment and more about social attitudes, interpretations of disability, architectural barriers, legal barriers, and educational barriers." The first "independent living center" in Berkeley, in the 1970s, provided an array of services, all performed by disabled peers: peer counseling, advocacy, van transportation, training in living skills, wheelchair repair, housing referral, attendant care referral.

During the last 30 years, there was significant growth of public spending on disability programs. In parallel was the growth of parent and consumer advocacy and the "disability business." About 46% of the funding supported placement of persons with disabilities in segregated settings such as nursing homes, sheltered workshops, and mental institutions.

"Advocacy by specific, single-disability groups in the US began to evolve into cross-disability coalition building in the 1970s, 1980s, and 1990s and secured passage of ADA."

> Braddock, D. & Parish, S. (2001). An institutional history of disability. In G. Albrecht, K. Seelman & M. Bury (Eds.), *Handbook of Disability Studies* (pp. 11-68). Thousand Oaks, CA: Sage.

Early trends in the U.S. toward institution-based services are being repeated in developing countries, as they move from agrarian economies toward urbanization. They echo our patterns from the 19th Century into the 20th.

"Specialized, institution-based services are often the first type of organized assistance instituted in developing countries. They are impairment specific, with schools for blind children among the first to be established. Usually they are started by organizations in the colonizing country, often on a religious or philanthropic basis."

"Specialized institutions sometimes became places for minimal care and confinement. (This was especially true of mental institutions… depositories for people considered dangerous or whose families could not keep them.)"

Institutions typically were underfunded and had to be selective. They added external services when capacity was a problem.

Community-based rehabilitation is the alternative, and it is the dominant recent approach in developing countries. The World Health Organization developed a plan to integrate rehabilitation services into local-level health care.

> Whyte, S.R. & Ingstad, B. (1995). Disability and culture: An overview. In B. Ingstad & S.R. Whyte (Eds.), *Disability and culture* (pp. 3-34). Berkeley: University of California Press.

A special issue of *Social Science and Medicine* represents the emergence of anthropological research on disability.

> Whyte, S.R. & Ingstad, B. (1995). Disability and culture: An overview. In B. Ingstad & S.R. Whyte (Eds.), *Disability and culture* (pp. 3-34). Berkeley: University of California Press.

21st CENTURY

"The issues become increasingly contentious as the discourse moves across national boundaries, disability types, and societal reactions." – G.D. Albrecht, K.D. Seelman, & M. Bury

A major paradigm shift is occurring in the definition of disability, due to globalization. Global communications, medicine, and economics are merging national views and cultures.

Disability Studies are emerging with roots in social sciences, humanities, and rehabilitation sciences. Organizations such as Rehabilitation International, the Society for Disability Studies, the British Council of Disabled People, the U.S. National Institute on Disability and Rehabilitation Research emerged. Academic Disability Studies programs offer degrees. The field has strong theoretical, applied, and social policy origins.

"The issues become increasingly contentious as the discourse moves across national boundaries, disability types, and societal reactions."

> Albrecht, G.D., Seelman, K.D., & Bury, M. (2001). The formation of Disability Studies. In G. Albrecht, K. Seelman & M. Bury (Eds.), *Handbook of Disability Studies* (pp. 1-7). Thousand Oaks, CA: Sage.

States have been closing training centers or large residential facilities for profoundly disabled people, moving them into community homes. Eleven states have yet to follow the path of deinstitutionalization. Some parents advocate continuing the availability of large facilities, others argue for community care, in the form of group homes.

The number of people housed in institutions nationally fell from 186,743 in 1970, to 84,239 in 1990, to 33,000 now – reduced by a factor of 5-6 since 1970.

It costs Virginia an average of $181,000 a year to care for a resident in a training center, whereas community care costs $110,000 to $143,000.

There are long waiting lists for community care or small group homes, and the default situation is family. For example, in Virginia, 5,000 people are on a waiting list for five training centers housing 1,150 people now. Older family caregivers worry about replacing themselves.

> Cauvin, H.E. (2010, July 22). State facilities for the mentally disabled are all some families have. *The Washington Post*.

The 20th Century transformed the experience of persons with disability and their treatment. We do not yet live in a social environment free of discrimination or free of physical and communications barriers, but legal rights and public policies are in place and much thinking has shifted.

"In the past, the emphasis was to provide support to people with disabilities primarily through [income] benefits. Today the emphasis has shifted to supporting independence and promoting involvement in all aspects of society."

> U.S. Census Bureau (2010). Overview.
> http://www.census.gov/hhes/www/disablity/overview.html

The Disability Rights Movement

"[People with disabilities] became proactive in defining their own needs, asserting themselves as consumers, not as patients, and working to change legislation and attitudes." -N.B. Miller & C.C. Sammons

OVERVIEW

During a few decades starting in the early 1970s, a great transformation occurred in the lives of people with disabilities in the U.S. We can characterize the change as follows:

BEFORE
- Residence in institutions isolated from the community
- Patronization by caretakers ("the helping industry")
- Many physical barriers to mobility in public places
- No accommodation for deafness or blindness in public areas
- Limited employment options
- Exclusion from public presence
- No persons with disabilities teaching or running institutions for disabled people
- Small advocacy organizations for a few subgroups (blind, deaf, some diseases)

AFTER
- National advocacy organizations; self-advocacy; strong parent groups
- Removal of physical barriers in public places, by law
- Public transportation designed for assistance
- Ban on employment discrimination, by law
- Signage and interfaces for hard of hearing and visually impaired people
- Entrance into professional positions in general
- Jobs as teachers and administrators serving disabled people open up
- Assistive technologies research and products flourish
- Rise of independent living centers and support networks
- Biographical and anthropological testimonials about life with a disability
- Rise of the field of Disability Studies
- Rise of special education in schools, integrated into mainstream
- National identity for persons with disabilities as a group and as a movement

ORIGINS

There are three common conditions leading to the social movements of the sixties (civil rights, women's rights, welfare rights, student protest, disability rights movements). First, there is a preexisting wide communications network. Second, the network is receptive to a new idea. Third, a crisis galvanizes the network into organizing around the new idea.

> Freeman, J. (1999). On the origins of social movements. In Freeman, J. & Johnson, V. (Eds.) *Waves of protest: social movements since the sixties*. NY: Rowman & Littlefield.

In the case of the disability rights movement, these conditions converged.

After the passage of the Vocational Rehabilitation Act in 1973, people with disabilities were heartened by the promise of the new law. It was a milestone in public policy. It banned discrimination, encouraged affirmative action in hiring, mandated "reasonable accommodation" and accessibility to public places, public transport, and public communications systems.

Federal action on the law was slow, and even stalled due to lack of commitment on the part of the current administration, and fear of the cost of implementing "reasonable accommodation." Normally, a law is translated into regulations shortly after the law is passed, and then government entities enforce the law.

A coalition of groups lobbying for disability rights in Washington wrote a letter in 1977 (four years after the law had been passed) to President Jimmy Carter, threatening a national protest if Secretary Joseph Califano Jr. did not proceed to enforce the Vocational Rehabilitation Act, first by signing new regulations. Sit-ins were held in ten different cities. They were small and short, except the demonstrations in San Francisco.

A social movement was already congealing around the Berkeley Center for Independent Living (CIL), the first of its kind established in 1972. Berkeley had become a de facto "capital for the handicapped." The Berkeley CIL created a "504 Emergency Coalition." ("504" was the section of the law pertaining to "reasonable accommodation.") Its demonstration was echoed around the country and aligned with the 45 groups belonging to the American Coalition of Citizens With Disabilities (ACCD). In the Bay area, labor organizations, the Salvation Army, an ex-prisoner organization and others contributed money and food to keep the demonstrators in action for twenty-four days.

Califano's bureaucratic manipulations and avoidance of signing the regulations provided the focal point. The independent living programs growing in California brought together like-minded activists with an independent living philosophy. The rallying supporters included media and congressmen, as well as other groups across the country. There was a long dramatic sit-in by people with disabilities at Berkeley that attracted national attention. Califano finally signed the regulations in April, 1977, on the 24th day of the sit-in.

The long San Francisco sit-in galvanized group identity and consciousness among persons with disabilities. Members of this group were relatively much more isolated from each other than women and racial minorities. It was physically and socially more difficult for them to convene. They were fragmented into subcultures, for example, deaf and blind people. The "504 Takeover" represented a common civil rights struggle, across types of disabilities. Even Califano referred to the appearance of a new era of civil rights. The movement was aligned and associated with the other social movements for rights. The Berkeley Center and its action tended to de-stigmatize disability, built group identity, and gave members a sense of power.

At the time, there was no national social movement or network at the time. There were small local organizations of activists, such as the League of the Physically Handicapped in New York. The focus of the 1973 Act was vocational rehabilitation, not civil rights. It followed a series of rehabilitation acts, starting after World War I to accommodate returning wounded veterans and help them get jobs. These laws spelled out services of job training, counseling, and job placement. There were rehabilitation acts after World War II also, after the Korean War, and after the war in Vietnam. But the legislative philosophy shifted in 1973.

Section 504 stated: "No otherwise qualified handicapped individual in the United States, shall solely by reason of his handicap, be excluded from the participation in, be denied the benefits of, or be subjected to discrimination under any program or activity receiving Federal financial assistance."

The wording thus stated a commitment to the *rights* of disabled people. It paralleled the language of Section 601 of Title VI of the 1964 Civil Rights Act and Title IX of the 1972 Education Amendments Act. None of these laws guaranteed implementation and compliance.

Johnson, R.A. (1999). Mobilizing the disabled. In Freeman, J. & Johnson, V. (Eds.). *Waves of protest: social movements since the sixties*. NY: Rowman & Littlefield.

INDEPENDENT LIVING MOVEMENT

The Berkeley Center for Independent Living put together an array of services that made it possible for people in wheelchairs with multiple impairments to live without residential caretakers, and go to work. It provided peer counseling, advocacy, van transportation, training in living skills, wheelchair repair, housing referral, and attendant care referral.

Its leaders identified four core principles for independent living: self-determination, self-image and public education, advocacy, service to all. By 2000, there were 336 centers and 253 subordinate sites serving 212,000 people.

The advocacy organization Disabled in Action was founded in 1970. In 1972 it had 15,000 members. They conducted a March on Washington, held protests at inaccessible buildings, and demonstrated against Jerry Lewis' MS telethons which featured cute children in need of help. Disabled in Action led to the formation in 1974 of the American Coalition of Citizens with Disabilities, the umbrella organization for disability advocate groups across the nation.

Self-advocacy by people with mental illness organized in opposition to organized psychiatry, psychotropic medication, and institutional treatment. They opposed involuntary, uninformed use of electroconvulsive therapy (ECT) and in general, treatment without the consent of the patient.

Deaf students at Gallaudet University advocated for a deaf president in 1988. They also sought a deaf majority on the university's board. The first deaf president of Gallaudet was appointed as a result of their protest.

> Braddock, D. & Parish, S. (2001). An institutional history of disability. In G. Albrecht, K. Seelman & M. Bury (Eds.), *Handbook of Disability Studies* (pp. 11-68). Thousand Oaks, CA: Sage.

SELF-DETERMINATION AND IDENTITY

Fundamental shifts in thinking occurred in our society. The prevailing thinking before the 1970s (and persisting still) is that disability is a medical condition, diagnosed by medical practitioners who determined what a person with a certain impairment could do or not do in daily life. The new thinking focused on *what people could do if they had the right conditions.*

The movement "redefined independence ... as the quality of one's life with help."

"The medical model of disability measured independence by how far one could walk after an illness or how far one could bend his legs after an accident. But Ed Roberts redefined independence as the control a disabled person had over his life. Independence was measured not by the tasks one could perform without assistance but by the quality of one's life with help."

One of the consequences of this thinking was action on the part of people with disabilities to take back control over who they were and what they could do. A group identity emerged from the diverse population. "They became proactive in defining their own needs, asserting themselves as consumers, not as patients, and working to change legislation and attitudes."

> Miller, N. B. & Sammons, C.C. (1999). *Everybody's Different: Understanding and Changing Our Reactions to Disabilities*. Baltimore: Paul H. Brookes Pub. Co.

INCLUSION NOT ISOLATION

"Throughout history, the separation of people with disabilities has been a common practice. Because disabilities were frequently thought to be linked with moral or spiritual failings, families typically felt a great deal of shame. …

In the 1960s and 1970s, a dramatic shift in our society's philosophy led to the recognition that people with mental retardation needed and wanted to live in the community and participate in all aspects of daily life, including education, work, recreation, and voting. This movement, known as *normalization*, coincided with the Kennedy administration's support, the exposure of substandard institutional care, and the growing empowerment of parents who insisted on raising their children at home with essential services and supports."

"In the 1980s and 1990s, people with disabilities, professionals, parents, and others have forged alliances to articulate the needs of people with disabilities and to work toward common goals of increasing social awareness, advocating for disability rights in education and employment, and making communities more accessible for people with special needs. This focus, known as *inclusion,* emphasizes that people with disabilities have the right to full community participation and that communities have the responsibility to ensure equal access to full community participation."

> Miller, N. B. & Sammons, C.C. (1999). *Everybody's Different: Understanding and Changing Our Reactions to Disabilities*. Baltimore: Paul H. Brookes Pub. Co.

PERSONAL TESTIMONY RAISES AWARENESS

Social science studies, with their focus on the experience and perspective of the informant, generated more accounts of the experience of disability. How did people with disabilities view their own situation? How did they live with an impairment? We start to read about the lives of mentally retarded people, people with multiple sclerosis, or people living without limbs.

Irving Zola, a medical sociologist who normally used a cane, tried living in a wheelchair in a village for disabled people in Holland and wrote an account. Robert Murphy, an anthropologist, describes his experience of becoming paralyzed, with the writing delivered as a product of anthropological field research. Michael Dorris writes about the life of his adopted son who had fetal alcohol syndrome. Thus we have "afflicted participant- observers" using the tools of their profession to interpret cultural difference.

> Whyte, Susan Reynolds (1995). Disability between discourse and experience. In B. Ingstad & S.R. Whyte (Eds.), *Disability and culture* (pp. 267-291). Berkeley: University of California Press.

DISABILITY STUDIES, "PERSONS WITH DISABILITIES," AMERICANS WITH DISABILITIES ACT

Disability became a new political and cultural identity in the 1970s. The earliest writings in "Disability Studies" appear in the 1970s and 1980s. The entity "persons with disabilities" and "Deaf people" appear. The return of veterans from the war in Vietnam energized the disability rights movement which culminated in the Americans with Disabilities Act of 1990. The "charity" and "medical" models were replaced with the civil rights and social models.

With the Americans With Disabilities Act of 1990 (ADA), there are protections against discrimination, and also a definition of who is eligible to enjoy those protections. The category of disability still has ambiguities and lacks coherence, for example, including conditions such as "obesity, attention deficit disorder, diabetes, back pain, carpal tunnel syndrome, severe facial scarring, chronic fatigue syndrome, skin conditions" and so on. "Is there a core identity there?"

The feeling that the protected class is too large is possibly behind a backlash to the ADA. People with minor conditions are asking to be considered disabled and in need of accommodation. About 95 percent of cases before the courts claiming rights under ADA are denied. This confounds the struggle for equal rights and accommodation in housing, jobs, and public facilities.

With ADA the category "disabled" has grown large and complex, and *unstable*.

Class is also a factor. The majority of people with disabilities are poor, unemployed, and undereducated. "Only one-third of people with disabilities are employed, versus upward of 70 percent of 'normal' workers." Many people with cognitive and affective disabilities end up in prisons.

> Davis, L.J. (2010). The end of identity politics: On disability as an unstable category. In L.J. Davis (Ed.), *The Disability Studies reader* (3rd Ed.) (pp. 301-315). New York: Routledge

UNFINISHED BUSINESS

Clearly the objectives of the disability rights movement are not all realized yet. Social attitudes lag. Architectural and physical accommodations are not universal. Employers may not understand the law and options for reasonable accommodation or about the existence of assistive devices and software.

People with disabilities themselves may not have the energy, awareness, or interest to participate in collective advocacy. "Achieving inclusive societies will require persons with mental, physical, and sensory disabilities to learn more about one another and to construct more powerful ... cross-disability coalitions."

> Braddock, D. & Parish, S. (2001). An institutional history of disability. In G. Albrecht, K. Seelman & M. Bury (Eds.), *Handbook of Disability Studies* (pp. 11-68). Thousand Oaks, CA: Sage.

Is the Disability Rights Movement Similar to the Civil Rights and Women's Rights Movements?

If you remove social barriers and discrimination against women and minorities, they may flourish and participate. With disabled people, you have both social discrimination and physical environments that "discriminate." The design of most of our ordinary physical environments and tools assume a relatively narrow range of ability. There is great inertia in changing existing products and spaces.

COMMON INTERESTS

It is easy to imagine that civil rights were a common agenda among women, African Americans, and persons with disabilities, and that the movements occurred in parallel. All the rights movements sought to put in place laws that would ban discrimination and grant equal rights to housing, education, employment, and other public services. They benefited from the remedy of affirmative action in employment, which has undergone modification over time but followed a common principle from the beginning: making up for and reversing patterns of employment discrimination in the past.

All three movements were energized by the anti-war movement of the 1960's that questioned authority and the status quo.

UNIQUE INTERESTS

Persons with disabilities have unique interests in addition that were not on the agenda for able-bodied women and racial groups per se:

- A need for medical services to treat impairments that can be treated
- A need for rehabilitation services to recover the ability to function at home and at work
- Vocational training in order to enter or re-enter the job market
- A personal voice in the choice of medical treatments
- Physical modifications in public spaces (doors, ramps, bathrooms, voting booths) and in public transportation to enable greater mobility
- Physical modifications that are called for in many small business locations such as restaurants, banks, stores, stadiums, etc.
- Reasonable accommodation that may require special knowledge on the part of employers
- Design features in electronic information systems for poor vision or hearing
- A right to healthy and safe treatment in institutions
- Special education, with specialized teachers, individual learning plans, physical facilities, and practices sensitive to regulations
- Access to mainstream education in schools and colleges
- The right to live independently in the community, with help

The need for structural changes and accommodations in the standard design of our physical environment and tools is one of the biggest differences. Discrimination is "institutionalized" in our physical infrastructures.

GROUP IDENTITY

The characteristics of gender and skin color are usually immutable. That is, you are born with them (for the most part) and are not likely to "exit" from the group.

Persons with disabilities can "join" the group, and "exit" from it. While "in the group," a person with a disability may want to keep the impairment private, especially if it is invisible (for example, cancer).

People with disabilities might live in institutions by necessity, or at home. Depending on the severity and nature of their impairment, they may live fairly isolated from public and community participation. Thus "group identity" is not strong and reinforced through interaction with others sharing a particular impairment or any impairment.

Another big difference in the rights movements was that people with disabilities were fragmented, as a community, into groups around particular impairments. "Cross-disability" identity had to develop.

The gatekeepers for becoming a person with a disability are medical practitioners. Eligibility for many benefits and services require certification by a physician. Physicians' diagnoses may change over time, for example, particularly in the definitions of mental illnesses.

The assessments of medical and educational practitioners can be biased, and cloud the truth of impairment. For example, more boys are placed in special education, more African American men are incarcerated in prisons rather than treated for addictions or mental illness, wild teenagers and difficult spouses can be pushed into treatment. Diagnoses can be politicized. Treatment can be involuntary and forced. Women and racial minorities are not as likely to be "cast" or "labeled" into their group.

Some impairments require the personal assistance of a caregiver either for certain tasks in the course of a day, or constantly. Dependency itself is stigmatized in our society as a sign of weakness and powerlessness. Regardless of the nature of the impairment, then, there is some stigma to be overcome (and possibly shame) from needing a human hand.

On the other hand, some impairments are invisible. If someone is unemployed, they might be subjected to social stigma, with the implicit question of whether they are deserving of charity and public welfare.

In short, people with disabilities do not form an obvious identity group. There are many different types of impairments with different implications for dependence, stigma, work, and options for assistance. Many choose not to self-identify with the "group" because of stigma.

> Lewis, B. (2010). A mad fight: Psychiatry and disability activism. In L.J. Davis (Ed.), *The Disability Studies reader* (3rd Ed.) (pp. 160-176). New York: Routledge.

"Impairment raises moral and metaphysical problems about personhood, responsibility, and the meaning of differences. Questions about autonomy and dependence, capacity and identity, and the meaning of loss are central."

> Whyte, S.R. & Ingstad, B. (1995). Disability and culture: An overview. In B. Ingstad & S.R. Whyte (Eds.), *Disability and culture* (pp. 3-34). Berkeley: University of California Press.

Being female, or having a different sexual orientation, or having a different skin pigmentation or body shape are issues of identity and discrimination. If you remove social discrimination against these groups, they flourish and participate.

In T. Shakespeare's view, with disabled people, you have both discrimination and real limitations. If all *social* barriers were removed, the impaired person does not become advantaged or equally enabled.

He believes that it is harder to celebrate disability as an identity. Disability is limitation and incapacity. It is not necessarily a condition and an identity from birth.

Finally, removing social discrimination is not sufficient. It takes resources to change our structural environments to meet the needs of a wide range of disabled people, because traditional constructions and transportation systems were built with features that render them inaccessible.

> Shakespeare, T. (2010). The social model of disability. In L.J. Davis (Ed.), *The Disability Studies reader* (3rd Ed.) (pp. 266-273). New York: Routledge.

People with invisible disabilities are often reluctant to self-identify, or identify with the movement, to avoid stigma and stereotyping.

Unlike gender or race, the attribute of "disability" or "impairment" is not clear-cut or visible. A wide range of impairments are lumped together in the phrase "persons with disabilities." Each individual encounters unique circumstances, in terms of the implication for functioning in society. Our approach to special education has recognized that "one size does not fit all" for children with impairments, and each requires his or her own plan based on needs. There are degrees of "difference," stigma, and challenge. The individual's experience, and society's response to that individual, is not as predictable as it might be based on gender or race.

USUALLY NO SOCIALIZATION OR PREPARATION FOR THE STATUS

Disability is unlike other stigmatized conditions. It is a position that can be acquired by anyone. Persons with disabilities typically are not reared by disabled parents, nor did many grow up among disabled people. It is not a culture into which they were socialized. Often the newly-disabled person must be re-socialized as they are rehabilitated, and the process alienates their parents who remain ignorant of their experience of rehabilitation and new rules. "The very essence of most disability is that it represents a sharp interruption, and commonly a reversal, of fortunes…. As such, the disabled are less comparable to African Americans and Asians, who were always black or Asian."

Their status is shared, conceivably, with people who have suffered an acute loss of income and status. They too go through a "mourning period" and enter a "fall from grace" as they enter a life of adversity and ambiguity.

Murphy, Robert F., Scheer, Jessica, Murphy, Yolanda, & Mack, Richard (1988). Physical disability and social liminality: A study in the rituals of adversity. *Social Science and Medicine*, 26(2), 235-242.

ROLE OF PARENTS

Parents of children with disabilities have played a large role in activism. A number of national advocacy organizations (around certain disabilities) are motivated by parents' interests in services for their children. This is a big difference between the disability rights movement and the others.

Communication with Phil Calkins and Jean Sando, December 2010.

INTENSITY OF GOVERNMENT INTERVENTION

Besides the medical and education professions in defining disability, the need for special services inevitably means that the government plays a large role in the life of a person with disabilities.

"Public policies not only reflect social status and cultural constructs; they also help create and reinforce them. This active governmental role has especially applied to disabled people, whose exclusion from much of mainstream economic life, along with the need by some for accommodation for their impairments, creates a greater need for public services and subsidies. Much of the social construction of disability and its consequences in the past hundred years has come through the medium of public policymaking and policy implementation." "... define who may work and who may receive public subsidies if they do not work; who may attend school and what services they will receive when they get to school; and whether people with disabilities have access to public transportation and private telecommunication systems."

> Scotch, Richard K. (2001). American disability policy in the 20th Century. In P.K. Longmore & L. Umansky (Eds.) *The new disability history: American perspectives* (pp. 375-392). New York: New York University Press.

DIFFERENT ORIGINS

On the positive side, the first impetus for the disability rights movement was not a campaign to get legislation passed, but to get the Federal government to *implement* and *enforce* the legislation.

The movement was not focused on getting legislation passed, like the women's and the civil rights movements. The federal government in effect facilitated the disabilities movement by recognizing and legitimizing rights in the 1973 Act. The movement came out of a demand for implementation of the law.

> Johnson, R.A. (1999). Mobilizing the disabled. In Freeman, J. & Johnson, V. (Eds.). *Waves of protest: social movements since the sixties.* NY: Rowman & Littlefield.

Getting the regulations deriving from the Vocational Rehabilitation Act of 1973 signed (in 1977) was only the beginning of intensive activism and an intensive sequence of public policy milestones. During the heat of activism by the independent living movement, the Education for All Handicapped Children Act was passed in 1975. Later the Americans With Disabilities Act (1990) and the Individuals with Disabilities Education Act (2004) solidified and clarified rights and led to the provision of significant services.

Sympathy for wounded war veterans and interests in child welfare might have made it easier to get legislation passed. There is more controversy in affirmative action for women and minorities, for example. The Equal Rights Amendment that would give women equal rights under the law is still not part of the U.S. Constitution. It was proposed in 1923, passed out of Congress in 1972, was ratified by 35 of 38 needed states, and is still pending passage.

What is the Experience of Persons with Disabilities?

"We believe the person with a stigma is not quite human. ... We effectively, if often unthinkingly, reduce his life chances." – Erving Goffman

Personal accounts of the experience of having an impairment started appearing in the 18th Century. In the 20th Century, many published accounts led to an appreciation for the social and emotional circumstances society inflicts on disabled people.

An early account of the experience of disability was written by William Hay in 1754. His essay, called *Deformity*, describes the effect of his impairment (a bent back) on his life. He notes that his high social class protected him from the "insolence" of society.

> Barnes, Colin (2010). A brief history of discrimination and disabled people. In L.J. Davis (Ed.), *The Disability Studies reader* (3rd Ed.) (pp. 20-32). New York: Routledge.

Disabled people are still a focus of comedy. This treatment harks back to the Middle Ages, where impairment was a source of amusement. The higher classes visited Bedlam to laugh at "idiots."

> Barnes, Colin (2010). A brief history of discrimination and disabled people. In L.J. Davis (Ed.), *The Disability Studies reader* (3rd Ed.) (pp. 20-32). New York: Routledge.

There are many examples of literary and activist biographies. A notable example is the recent movie about Temple Grandin, based on her book. She is currently a scientist and a professor – thus transcending certain thresholds for authority and intelligence—who describes her experience as someone with autism. Her story—very popular in public speaking engagements-- not only informed researcher's views, but gave the public an "insider's view" and addressed many misperceptions.

> Dr. Temple Grandin's Official Website. http://www.templegrandin.com/ 2010.

A long list of books and videos of this type is available in the Miller and Sammons book.

> Miller, N. B. & Sammons, C.C. (1999). *Everybody's Different: Understanding and Changing Our Reactions to Disabilities*. Baltimore: Paul H. Brookes Pub. Co.

THE EXPERIENCE OF STIGMA

Erving Goffman's book *Stigma* posed a theory explaining the phenomenon of social exclusion of persons with disabilities, morally unearned. Stigma also applies to other characteristics such as race and religion that can be culturally devalued. Other sociologists use the word "deviance" and "otherness." He contributed the idea of social rejection due to shame – not just social rejection due to strangeness, in explaining the deep dynamics in our treatment of persons with disabilities.

Some modern sociologists disagree that "stigma" is an adequate concept, but the book remains a classic in Disability Studies.

Goffman's book contains dozens of personal accounts from persons with disabilities. For example, blind people who are not supposed to make jokes, or enjoy dancing.

He says that the idea of stigma, or disgrace and shame associated with disability, has origins in the Christian Middle Ages. Physical mutilation, including blinding, was a punishment for certain crimes, especially among the Normans and the French. Natural blindness was considered a punishment by God. Earlier, the Greeks branded or scarred slaves, criminals, and traitors. The marked person was morally bad.

According to Goffman (citation below), society categorizes people as ordinary and natural, or not, based on certain characteristics and expectations. These categories become unconscious and automatic. In usual discourse, we normally expect certain characteristics, and they comprise a virtual social identity. However, a person who does not have ordinary characteristics will be perceived as tainted, or bad, dangerous, or weak. His actual social identity may have attributes that are viewed as negative, and these evoke stigma, or shame. Stigma is a social dynamic; not an inherent quality of the victim. People having a tainted social identity may try to hide characteristics that mark them as failures or outsiders.

There are three different types of stigma. First, due to various physical deformities. Second, due to qualities of character such as dishonesty, addiction, or unemployment.

Finally, there are stigmas of race, nation, and religion which can be transmitted through lineages and are associated with whole groups, categorically. (We might add sexual orientation to the list now.)

"By definition, we believe the person with a stigma is not quite human. On this assumption we exercise varieties of discrimination, through which we effectively, if often unthinkingly, reduce his life chances." We use specific stigma terms such as "cripple," "bastard," and "moron." We have theories that explain the inferiority of the person with a stigma.

"The central feature of the stigmatized individual's situation in life ... is a question of 'acceptance.' Those who have dealings with him fail to accord him the respect and regard…. he anticipates." The victim internalizes the stigma, finding things wrong with himself and feeling self-hate. As one said, looking in a mirror, "I saw a stranger, a little, pitiable, hideous figure."

The stigmatized individual tries to compensate for the deficiency, or correct it, by mastering activities felt to be out of his range, for example, a blind person skiing or mountain climbing. He tries to belong where he is not expected to belong. He tries to assimilate into normal acceptance. [Modern scholars might say is the motivation is not compensation and proving anything, but about fun.]

The stigma interferes with social interactions by introducing uncertainty and throwing both parties off balance. "The blind, the ill, the deaf, the crippled can never be sure what the attitude of a new acquaintance will be." The victim of stigma is an unusual and unpredictable person. Is he human? Is he like normal people in interests, likes, dislikes?

As Goffman puts it, the stigma "spoils his social identity" and cuts him off from society.

Sometimes a person with a stigma is socially successful – that is, attains a high position in spite of the barriers of his stigma. He may be put in a position of representing his stigmatized group – "look, he did it!" This reinforces his own stigma, reminding others of it even more, and draws others with the stigma to rally around him, further isolating him from normal acceptance. This is true also if the person breaks the law, wins a prize, or becomes the first of his kind in some way. The public media cannot resist drawing attention to the person's aspects that evoke the stigma.

Persons sharing a stigma may seek to socialize with each other for escape and mutual acceptance, as a relief from the tensions and ambiguities of being the "other" among "normals."

Public school is the place where stigmas are first learned. Children will taunt without inhibition, exercising newly learned rules of society.

The workplace is a battle field for negotiating acceptance among strangers. "Looking for a job was like standing before a firing squad. Employers were shocked that I had the gall to apply for a job."

People who become disabled later in life will re-identify themselves, finding "who he is going to have to be" because of the new disability and the new experience of stigma.

Goffman, Erving (1963). *Stigma: Notes on the management of spoiled identity*. NY: Simon & Schuster.

DEHUMANIZATION

Robert Murphy, an anthropologist who became a paraplegic in the 1980's, wrote about his experience from the professional view of a "participant observer."

"There is a clear pattern ... of prejudice towards the disabled and debasement of their social status. This is manifested in its most extreme forms by avoidance, fear, and outright hostility. ... The disabled occupy the same devalued status as ex-convicts, certain ethnic and racial minorities, and the mentally ill. ... The physically impaired person ... is given a negative identity by society, and much of his social life is a struggle against this imposed image. ... The greatest impediment to a person's taking full part in his society is not his physical flaws, but rather the tissue of myths, fears, and misunderstandings that society attaches to them."

America has made a fetish of the body, giving it magical powers. It must be kept very clean and lean. Obesity is evidence of sloth and a weak will, and lower-class status. The body must appear young. People with disabilities, unfortunately, contradict the values of youth, virility, activity and physical beauty. People with disabilities subvert the ideal "just as the poor betray the American Dream." People recoil from visible reminders of imperfection and reminders of their own vulnerability.

Many books written by disabled people protest the dehumanization they experience, for example, the classic book *And Yet We Are Human*.[30]

In Japan, the stigma of disability is worse and an "aura of contamination" attaches to other members of the family. There is a belief that disability is a punishment for something.

In America, a person with a disability becomes quasi-human and an alien species. "Social encounters are always tricky games, sparring matches in which each party tries to guess what the reaction of the other will be." A resolution to this tension is avoidance, for example, averting of the eyes. The able-bodied may have a fear of contamination. Many in the public will withdraw deference to the impaired person, unconsciously. For example, an airline ticket agent will address the attendant of even someone of stature like Itzhak Perlman; a waiter will take orders from someone else. Disabled people are treated as minors or as incompetent, even though their disability is only physical. Psychologically, an able-bodied individual is distancing him or herself to reduce the feeling of their own vulnerability. A disabled person finds himself on the periphery of society, pensioned off and largely out of sight, even inside a hospital. Franklin D. Roosevelt hid his paralysis from the public to counter this treatment and perception.

With a lack of clear cultural guidelines for behavior, a social interaction can be tense and forced, as each party struggles with ambiguity and resorts to becoming more formal or faking humor. Consciousness of awkwardness must be suppressed and disavowed. The impaired person must become an expert on putting others at ease. The able-bodied must pretend that the impairment makes no difference.

Murphy and a disabled friend organized a program on disabilities in a library and expected a large crowd. Few came. He realized former friends and neighbors were "repelled by the subject" and were now ambivalent toward him. "The old social me had died."

There is a temptation for the impaired person to socialize more with other fellow-outsiders. This poses new dynamics, for example, crossing usual lines of social status. The mutual identification leads to more spontaneous openness between people who without their disabilities might not interact.

---

[30] Carling, Finn. & Haecker, T. (1980). And yet we are human and Kierkegaard: the cripple. Ayer. Originally published in 1958, translated from Norwegian in 1962, and reprinted.

Murphy also found he had a new ease with women, because his identity as a man was overruled by his new identity as a paraplegic.

In the sociological literature, Murphy notes that people with disabilities find themselves falling into the category of the contaminated outsiders along with felons, minorities, deviants – those who have broken some taboo and are ritually polluted. The more the deviation from normal appearance, the more disturbing to the normal, for example, facial disfigurement is at the bottom of the scale. Restaurants used to turn away obviously impaired people, until laws and social mores changed.

> Murphy, Robert (1995). Encounters: The body silent in America. In B. Ingstad & S.R. Whyte (Eds.), *Disability and culture* (pp. 140-158). Berkeley: University of California Press. Originally published in 1987.

LIMINALITY, OR UNDEFINED STATUS

Erving Goffman in 1963 posed the idea that stigma explains the interactions between able-bodied people and people with disabilities. He suggested that because people with disabilities (at least visible disabilities) deviate from what is considered normal, their identity is "spoiled" and they are made into outsiders and made the objects of prejudice.

One objection to Goffman's model is that stigma is too inclusive. Social deviants of all kinds suffer stigma: most ethnic and racial minorities, homosexuals, drug users, criminals, the mentally ill, as well as the physically disabled. Women who enter the workplace may enter this category as well. "All that is left are heterosexual WASP men in reasonably good physical condition, and preferably over five-and-a-half feet tall." Among the stigmatized are those who have deliberately violated the moral order, and those who fall into it, or are born into their devalued status. The physically disabled "similarly acquire their limitations through either birth or the misfortunes of life," and sometimes people hold them partly responsible for their misfortune.

"Prejudice against the disabled violates our moral order in a fundamental way." Our values and laws require equal treatment and even a helping hand to people with physical disabilities. Prejudice serves no economic purpose or political interest. Disabled people are "victims without a cause." Despite being harmless, they can inspire fear and revulsion.

Later sociologists propose that a better model explaining social interactions is one that is drawn from the anthropological study of ritual. Studies of ritual introduced the concept of *liminality*, a social state in which an individual's identity is nullified or suspended. During rites of passage in a society, the initiates are separated from society. They are taken through initiations and then reincorporated into society in a new state. During the transitional or liminal stage, the individual is marginal to society. Their old identity is expunged and they do not have a new one. They are both vulnerable (without social classification), and socially dangerous. That is why, in many societies, people in a liminal stage are isolated and separated from society, under the tutelage of instructors who might wear masks to mute their own social attributes.

The isolation of people with physically disabilities is like the sequestering of initiates. They are in an in-between state, neither sick nor well, neither fully healthy nor dead. We see that these people are deliberately excluded, in some societies, and even shunned. They suffer a contamination of identity (in Goffman's phrase, a "spoiled" identity). They are often considered dirty, unclean, polluted, and thus subject to taboo. Unlike initiates, however, they are not in transition to a new state, and their state remains ambiguous and undefined. A person who cannot walk is neither a child nor an adult. He or she may be confined because of physical barriers, especially in economically depressed housing, rendering him "invisible."

People in rehabilitation settings especially typify liminality. They are told what to do and have special rules and regimes. Usual interactions are suspended in the therapeutic environment. Relationships between patients are egalitarian, as are those among initiates. They are asexual and handled by caretakers.

Liminality is shared, conceivably, with people who have suffered an acute loss of income and status. They too go through a "mourning period" and enter a "fall from grace" as they enter a life of adversity and ambiguity.

> Murphy, Robert F., Scheer, Jessica, Murphy, Yolanda, & Mack, Richard (1988). Physical disability and social liminality: A study in the rituals of adversity. *Social Science and Medicine*, 26(2), 235-242.

RESOLVING STRAINED INTERACTIONS

Another early sociological analysis (1961) by Fred Davis looked at the interpersonal dynamics and tried to make sense of them, calling it a process of "resolving strained interaction."

Davis says that, in social relations, people cast others in the role of the deviant based on race, sexual orientation, and visible impairments. The negative attribution on a person imposes social injury, affecting employment, friendship, courtship, sex, travel, recreation, residence, and education, and especially every-day sociability, or informal interaction. How do people with visible impairments cope with the implicit charge that they are deviant, i.e., not "normal," which strains their interaction? They "disavow the deviance" and seek to "normalize" their identity to others. They try to re-establish a socially acceptable, normal relationship and position.

There is a tendency, in the social interaction, for the "normal" to focus exclusively on the impairment. Usually in a social interaction, each person reacts to the whole person and multiple qualities of the person; they do not fixate on one feature or quality. In the case of a visibly impaired individual, however, the impairment becomes a focal point and undermines the interaction. It is taboo to acknowledge the distraction and both people try to disguise the strain.

Second, there are implicit boundaries for how much emotion we are allowed to express in a new social interaction. In an interaction between a "normal" and a person with a visible impairment, the "normal" is shocked, or taken by surprise, due to the dissonance between his suppressed inner feelings that are inappropriate (e.g., pity, fear, repugnance, avoidance) and the positive niceties that are appropriate and expected (pleasure, warm interest). Davis calls the extra flood of emotion an "inundation of expressive boundaries."

Third, the "normal" feels an unsettling discord between the other qualities of a disabled individual, such as his job, clothes, speech, intelligence, interests, and the impairment. This is a "contradiction of attributes" that intrudes. For example, the "normal" might say "How strange to find a pretty girl in a wheelchair." Reducing the disabled individual, narrowly and negatively, casts a pall on the interaction.

Finally, there is difficulty in assessing whether the two can "do things" together. All people with visible impairments are not alike, and therefore have no common group stereotype. The "normal" person may have limited experience with a particular impairment. Can they go to lunch, go for a walk, and go to a movie? How to approach the question? Is the "normal" just being polite? Are there false assumptions about the ability to join together in some activity?

Davis analyses what the person with a disability must do to compensate for these difficulties. First, he accepts the fiction, on the surface, that the two parties are equal. He plays down the focus on the impairment and does not allow it to rule his social identity. Second, he projects personal qualities that encourage the "normal" to identify with him, and "breaks through" the focus on the impairment so that the "normal" doesn't see it any more. He "normalizes" his identity – not "the guy in the wheelchair" but "so-and-so who is smart and funny." He might be especially attentive and sympathetic to the "normal" or charming associate. Finally, in building the relationship, the person with an impairment briefs the "normal" about how to behave and how to help, for example, whether to open doors, or push, or offer a hand. The "normal" is oriented to the needs of person with a disability, and their interaction is "normalized" – made automatic and easy.

This process of "disavowing deviance" and "normalizing strained social relations" is similar in other contexts, for example, when a person loses a job, breaks a leg, or suffers a death in the family, and usual social protocols are disrupted.

Davis, Fred (1961). Deviance disavowal: The management of strained interaction by the visibly handicapped. *Social Problems*, 9, 121-132.

Discrimination and Treatment of Persons With Disabilities

"The metaphors of deafness—of isolation and foreignness, of animality, of darkness and silence—are projections reflecting the needs and standards of the dominant culture, not the experiences of most deaf people." – D. Baynton

Below are brief summaries of papers from social history and social science in Disability Studies, selected to highlight significant issues.

STIGMA, OTHERNESS, DIFFERENCE

Historically, a stigma was a physical mark or tattoo on the skin of criminals, slaves or traitors to designate them as undesirable people to be shunned. Now it is a symbolic "mark" of shame and disgrace.

Psychologists find that anxiety about strangers is universal among infants. They usually outgrow it, but it becomes part of learned responses to people who are different in their social context. The reaction can combine fear, dislike and disgust. The reactions to particular groups of "others" are learned in early socialization and become automatic. Cognitively, we need to categorize and order our experience, especially social experience, and the categories can evolve into schemas and stereotypes. Not all are negative. Stigma is a form of negative stereotyping.

Stigmatized individuals experience the rejection as a threat to their identity. "Stigma is a social death." A single stigmatizing characteristic such as a criminal record can trump other positive qualities. The victim can experience social isolation and lowered expectations from the "insiders" of a society. They can try to "pass," hiding the "fault," so as not to be socially quarantined.

"Fear is what gives stigma its intensity and reality." Certain diseases such as cancer and HIV/AIDS elicit fear because the causes and courses of the diseases are unknown, and there is a fear of contagion. Children born with birthmarks, epilepsy, or a caul can suffer stigma, due to beliefs that they are divine markers of some kind. Individuals who are mentally retarded can frighten others because the others feel that someone who is mentally retarded is unpredictable and potentially aggressive.

During difficult economic periods, there is increased aggression toward stigmatized groups. "Some people are stigmatized for violating norms, whereas others are stigmatized for being of little economic or political value."

Not all "otherness" or "difference" is stigmatized. Stigmas reflect the value judgments of a dominant group, which determines (consciously or unconsciously) which human differences are undesired and devalued to the point of stigma.

Brown, L.M.C. (2010). Stigma: An enigma demystified. In L.J. Davis (Ed.), *The Disability Studies reader* (3rd Ed.) (pp. 179-192). New York: Routledge.

ACROSS CULTURES

Teratology is the study of congenital defects in Western medicine. More accurately, we should speak of ethno-teratology – the study of concepts of bodily defects and anomalies across cultures. For example, cultures in Southern Africa view certain abnormalities to be so severe that an infant is "not allowed to be human," including breech birth, cutting the upper teeth first, defecating while being born. Sometimes the child is considered less of a person, unclean, or dangerous, but also having supernatural powers. Twins often have special status and in some cultures might be killed or celebrated. There are myths to explain the origin of the anomaly. The Yaka in Zaire, for example, initiate disabled people into a cult which gives them a prescribed status and even privileges.

There are many studies of infanticide. In Kenya, "anomalous babies were seen as sources of evil and metaphysical danger." Parents however, are known to refuse to comply. In Brazil, there is the "doomed child syndrome," due to certain conditions, and the child is allowed to die from neglect. The mothers do not attribute human characteristics to the child, giving them psychological distance.

Studies of attitudes toward disabilities are *themselves* vulnerable to unconscious bias and projection of a paternalistic view of persons with disabilities. It is hard to view other cultures apart from assumptions operating in our own. Developers working internationally, health professionals, social workers, rehabilitation experts, and aid agencies might justify their own "help" by viewing persons with disabilities as people needing their help, and needing the kind of help they get in America (for example, institutionalization). "Representations of disability may be linked to a political agenda." They may project the "medical model" of thinking. There are examples of cultural groups that do not agree with the "help" offered.

> Whyte, Susan Reynolds (1995). Disability between discourse and experience. In B. Ingstad & S.R. Whyte (Eds.), *Disability and culture* (pp. 267-291). Berkeley: University of California Press.

INEQUALITY JUSTIFIED

Western political thought has sought to explain inequality between persons or groups, particularly gender, race, and ethnicity. It has rarely addressed disability.

Historically, "it has been justifiable to treat disabled people unequally," and, "the concept of disability has been used to justify discrimination against other groups by attributing disability to them." For example, women were denied suffrage because they were considered deficient—mentally, emotionally, and physically—compared with males. Certain races and immigrants were restricted because of their perceived tendency to "feeblemindedness" and other impairments. "Disability has functioned for all such groups as a sign of and justification for inferiority."

The metaphor of the "natural" versus the "monstrous" evolved, by the late 19th Century, into the concept of the "natural and normal." "The natural was good and right because it conformed to the intent or design of Nature or the Creator of nature." The idea of the "normal" rose with the rise of social sciences and statistics. The opposite of "normal" was "defective." Western notions of progress and evolution led to the connection of nonwhite races to people with disabilities – reversions to earlier evolutionary stages. Down's syndrome was called Mongolism because it was considered the result of a biological reversion to the Mongol race. Deaf children without training were "savages." The freak shows positioned together "primitives" and "defectives."

Disability played a role in the justification for slavery. To wit, African Americans lacked sufficient intelligence to participate equally and independently in society. A second line of argument was that African Americans were prone to become disabled if they were free. They (as slaves!) tended to have a high incidence of deafness and blindness, and mental disorders. Certain mental disorders were specifically attributed to slaves who were treated as equals (and confused) by their masters.

Similarly, women were at risk if they were granted suffrage. They were mentally and by disposition incapable of voting responsibly, and they were too frail to be exposed to politics.

Both women and African Americans were considered at risk of getting sick if they were subjected to education. Mothers would suffer atrophy of their reproductive organs if they were educated.

Thus women, and certain races and ethnic groups had "medical problems" that warranted unequal and separate treatment. Like persons with disabilities, they needed to be protected from equality and education.

Early American immigration policy (at the end of the 19th Century) sought to exclude immigrants thought to be undesirable because they were thought to be mentally and physically deficient. Immigration officials had the authority to assess disability and reject individuals, working fairly fast. People with epilepsy, or "unstable," or homosexual, or "feebleminded" were excluded. "The detection of physical disabilities was a major aspect of the immigration inspector's work." They looked for arthritis, asthma, bunions, deafness, deformity, flat feet, heart disease, hernia, hysteria, poor eyesight, spinal curvature, and varicose veins.

With eugenics, the definition of undesirable expanded to cover appearance. There were "ugly" ethnicities. What we currently call "negative racial or ethnic profiling" was rampant. The thinking was that they would contaminate the American "stock," be unemployable, and therefore become a burden.

Unfortunately, a political response to these arguments was that women, and African Americans, and others were NOT cognitively or emotionally limited, and NOT "idiots" and "lunatics." The response was to dissociate gender, race and ethnicity from disability, not to question the unequal treatment of those with true disabilities. The stigma was not opposed. The cultural construct that persons with disabilities were innately inferior remained unquestioned.

> Baynton, D.C. (2001). Disability and the justification of inequality in American history. In P.K. Longmore & L. Umansky (Eds.) *The new disability history: American perspectives* (pp. 33-57). New York: New York University Press.

MEDICAL VERSUS SOCIAL MODELS OF IMPAIRMENT

Thought about disabilities often characterizes a contrast between two paradigms. The first arose in the 19th and 20th centuries as doctors were called to certify who was eligible to be housed in the new institutions for the mentally ill, for blind people, and so on. *Physicians became and still are gate-keepers for special services*. The underlying premise of the "medical model" is that impairment is a medical condition (mental or physical) to be diagnosed and treated. The doctor is in the position of healer, or, one who points to potential rehabilitation.

The social model sees impairment as a function of the environment. Persons with certain disabilities are not inherently impaired. They have conditions that are not accommodated by our typical environments. Physical (e.g., for mobility) or communications barriers (e.g., for blind or deaf people) prevent the "normal" functioning of the individual. A person using a wheelchair can function in society and in the workplace if he or she can travel to a building, enter it, move to upper floors, use restrooms, enter rooms, etc. A blind person can use an ATM machine if they can communicate with it through Braille or sound.

The social model also sees societal attitudes as a root cause of disability. A person with a disability (e.g., a disfigurement, blindness) could function "normally" in social and work life if they were not treated with pity, fear, or panic.

> Davidson, M. (2010). Universal design: The work of disability in the age of globalization. In L.J. Davis (Ed.), *The Disability Studies reader* (3rd Ed.) (pp. 133-146). New York: Routledge.

SOCIAL MODEL

The view of disabled people as an oppressed group in society, with rights to inclusion, independence, and control over medical treatment is a phenomenon of the last three decades. The new view is called the social model of disability.

The social model distinguishes between impairment (physical limitations) and "disability" which is social exclusion and oppression. Our social goal should be to accept impairment and to remove disability. Impairment may not be cured, but disability can be mitigated by changes in our physical environment and changes in our social attitudes. We should mandate the removal of physical barriers, and advocate for anti-discrimination legislation and supports for independent living.

One of the challenges in disabilities policy is that each approach differs in the characteristics they count and classify. People thinking according to the medical model are focused on counting and classifying the number of people with impairments, looking to medical prevention of impairments, and focused on cure or rehabilitation (i.e., "making people normal").

"Civil rights, rather than charity or pity, are the way to solve the disability problem," according to the social model.

> Shakespeare, T. (2010). The social model of disability. In L.J. Davis (Ed.), *The Disability Studies reader* (3rd Ed.) (pp. 266-273). New York: Routledge.

REVOLT AGAINST PSYCHIATRY

The medical view of disability "directs the health care industry toward a near exclusive focus on individual biomedical cures." They seek to cure the individual, "abnormal" body and do not look to change the social environment in which that body lives.

Disability activists reframe disability as a "social restriction and oppression." They focus on the view that much of the suffering of "abnormal" bodies comes from social exclusion, isolation, and lack of opportunity. The imposition of stigma and oppression against disabled people is called "ableism" – the prejudice of able-bodied people against disabled people.

Persons with mental disabilities similarly charge our systems with "sanism" – the prejudice of the sane against the mentally ill. The consequences of this prejudice can go beyond unpleasant experience and discrimination in the workplace. A person diagnosed or charged with mental illness can be involuntarily committed to a mental hospital or facility and be forced to take medication.

Roots of the resistance to "sanism" are evident in the late-nineteenth century. For example, the Anti-Insane Asylum Society protested the complicity of the psychiatric establishment in subordinating women to their husbands. A "disobedient" wife could be labeled insane, and incarcerated, without appeal. More than one despotic regime has used mental hospitals as a means to incarcerate and punish political dissidents. Thus treatment is a disguise for control, imprisonment and punishment.

The Mad Pride movement began in the 1970s by activists who had bad experiences in psychiatric facilities – disrespect, disregard, unjustified confinement, verbal and physical abuse, and exclusion from decision-making about their treatment. There are many published stories of "the journey back" from involuntary institutionalization and treatment. They comprise a "psychiatric survivor" movement.

Mind Freedom International evolved from the Mad Pride movement. It advocates for a revolution in mental health care that emphasizes the rights of those diagnosed with mental illness, protests what it considers abuses and mistreatments, and promotes alternative treatments. It questions psychiatric labeling, and charges that psychiatric drugs are causing more mental illness, not curing it.

In the last 30 years, psychiatry moved toward a preference for neuroscience and genetics at the expense of psychological and behavioral approaches. The dominant clinical model is bio-psychiatry with an almost exclusive focus on biomedical diagnoses and pharmacological treatments. (The style of Freud's psychoanalysis is out.) Its "blockbuster" medication is Prozac, which came off patent between 1987 and 2002. Lewis says that almost one in four people in the U.S. were started on a Prozac-type drug between 1987 and 2002. At the same time, the profits of pharmaceutical companies boomed, as did pharmaceutical funding behind the new "scientific" psychiatry.

One of the messages of the Mad Pride movement became amplified in the disability rights community: "no forced treatment ever;" the right to choose one's doctors and medication; the right to choose places of care; the right to care.

Lewis, B. (2010). A mad fight: Psychiatry and disability activism. In L.J. Davis (Ed.), *The Disability Studies reader* (3rd Ed.) (pp. 160-176). New York: Routledge.
MindFreedom International (2010). http://www.mindfreedom.org

DISABILITY AS INEQUALITY, OR LOST EQUALITY

"A fundamental theme in the contemporary Western discourse on disability is the assumption of the desirability of equality." "Disability implies a deprivation or loss of a needed competency or qualification… This notion of loss is underlined by the response to disability, *rehabilitation*, which implies restoration to a previous condition. There is an underlying ideal of equality lost and restored, and of the *right* to be able to participate equally.

Whyte, S.R. & Ingstad, B. (1995). Disability and culture: An overview. In B. Ingstad & S.R. Whyte (Eds.), *Disability and culture* (pp. 3-34). Berkeley: University of California Press.

CROSS-CULTURAL VIEWS

Are people with impairments impaired people?" People with impairments suffer not only the impairment. They are also treated differently as people. They may be infantilized, that is, treated like children. They may be dehumanized. For example, a severely impaired child or adult may be called a "vegetable." Infants born with many defects (and usually expected to die) can be treated as if they were not human. The folklore about changelings, or "strange children," often refers to abnormal characteristics or other-worldly origins. Twins are not considered human in Borneo, nor children born with teeth by the Bariba.

A recurring theme in the definition of personhood in Western civilizations is autonomy and independence. Excessive dependence and helplessness is associated with being child-like.

Socially, there may be different consequences for men and women. Women are expected to be more physically attractive generally, than men, and more nurturing in a marriage, and this might explain why disabled women are less likely to marry. In some cultures, it is important for adults to have children to achieve full status and respect. In cultures that value dowries or bride-wealth in marriage arrangements, a disabled woman may require a higher dowry or yield a lower bride-price.

Having a disability from birth or early youth has different consequences for social identity than becoming disabled later in life. Someone who has a chance to establish an independent social and economic position first is less likely to be defined by a later-occurring impairment. By extension, the disabilities that arise in old age are considered more "normal," and less stigmatizing.

A family's socio-economic status can make a difference in a community's treatment of a disabled child. A disabled child who is also poor is more likely to be teased and humiliated, having his physical or mental disability compounded by the social disability of poverty.

All of these negative concepts are reinforced by the media, the clergy, health personnel, and development agencies. Literary treatments also draw on and reinforce cultural views. However, public perception can be influenced to change in a positive direction through the same media and venues.

> Whyte, S.R. & Ingstad, B. (1995). Disability and culture: An overview. In B. Ingstad & S.R. Whyte (Eds.), *Disability and culture* (pp. 3-34). Berkeley: University of California Press.

INTERNATIONAL INEQUALITY

We need to consider disability as a global or international phenomenon. The view in the West assumes the rights of individuals and equality guaranteed by legal contract. But the ability of any country or society to improve access and employment presumes economic stability, and political stability. We need to consider class and the unequal distribution of wealth underlying the condition of persons with disabilities.

Economic processes can create more disability. For example, in 1984, the Bayer unit of Cutter Biological had a large stock of blood products for hemophiliacs that were unsaleable in the United States and Europe due to standards. They sold the tainted product in Asia and Latin America, leading to "a worldwide HIV infection rate of 90% among severe hemophiliacs and a four million dollar profit for Bayer." The recipients of blood transfusions became "collateral damage" in worldwide trade that is missing international standards and controls.

Western assumptions need to be revisited from a multi-cultural view, as we tend to export our solutions to places where they don't fit. Globally, we need to view disability as a matter of human rights rather than a healthcare problem.

> Davidson, M. (2010). Universal design: The work of disability in the age of globalization. In L.J. Davis (Ed.), The Disability Studies reader (3rd Ed.) (pp. 133-146). New York: Routledge.

NORMALCY AND THE RISE OF EUGENICS

The concept of what it is to have a "normal" body grew during the mid-19th Century. The word "normal" enters the English language around 1840-1860, referring to "common," "regular," or "usual."

Before we had the idea of "the normal," we had the concept of "the ideal" form of the body. By definition an ideal body is unattainable; it is an abstraction. It was the rise of statistics that introduced the concept of "normal." A French statistician, Adolphe Quetelet (1796-1847) proposed that "the average man" is a composite of the range of human attributes (height, weight, etc.) in a population. He also formed the idea of the middle class. Both were a kind of ideal, but based on real phenomena. In this construct, people with disabilities are considered deviants from the norm.

Interest in statistics first flourished in England in the 1830s. The Royal London Statistical Society was founded in 1835. We can appreciate the far-reaching impact of gathering numbers about everything. However, there was a symbiotic relationship between the foundation of statistics and the foundation of eugenics (the study of methods to improve the human race by selective breeding to eliminate undesirable genetic qualities).

The mid-century was also the time of the rise of Darwinism and the idea of the survival of the fittest. There was the idea that a population could be made "more normal" (and better) by eliminating or reducing deviant or "defective" outliers, even whole "nonstandard populations" such as deaf and blind people, people with physical imperfections, etc.

The term "eugenics" was introduced by Sir Francis Galton (1822-1911) who wanted to "fingerprint" individuals, looking for an essential marker or identity, capturing physical characteristics, for every individual, that he suspected were passed on through parentage. We later found these markers in genes, not fingerprints. He was interested in perfecting the human race, by identifying positive and negative extremes, including IQ. He contributed the ideas of the "normal distribution curve" and "intelligence quotient" (IQ).

The concern about "defectives" resonated elsewhere. In 1883, Alexander Graham Bell warned that deaf-mutes would marry other deaf-mutes and yield a race of deaf people (in *Memoir upon the Formation of a Deaf Variety of the Human Race*), which he considered a dire consequence.

Thus several trends -- the development of statistics, the theory of evolution, and interests in calibrating characteristics of humans -- converged with interests in perfecting the human race by controlling the reproductive rights of those having undesirable traits such as deafness. An early argument for birth control called for controlling the reproduction of paupers, syphilitics, epileptics, dipsomaniacs, "cripples," criminals, and degenerates.

Unfortunately, eugenics "became the common practice of many, if not most, European and American citizens." Also unfortunately, people with disabilities were lumped with other "unfit and undesirables" such as criminals.

There was preoccupation with identifying and cataloging forms of "errors" in the human race. Characteristics such as "feeblemindedness" and low intelligence were associated with certain ethnic groups, for example European immigrants to America.

"The loose association between what we would now call disability and criminal activity, mental incompetence, sexual license, and so on established a legacy that people with disabilities are still having trouble living down."

Literature of that time (Flaubert, Zola, Conrad) and even now exploits the idea of the Other as the "abnormal" and disabled. Characters who have something wrong with them morally might also be deaf, dumb, blind, or deformed.

It is a challenge in modern times to redefine the perception of "normal" so that physical differences are not also ideological. That is, so that physical disability is not considered "wrong."

> Davis, L.J. (2010). Constructing normalcy. In L.J. Davis (Ed.), *The Disability Studies reader* (3rd Ed.) (pp. 3-19). New York: Routledge.

ABORTION AND STERILIZATION, EUGENICS

Preventing the birth of "undesirables" through sterilization of selected groups was a clear agenda of the eugenics movement. In parallel, the practice of abortion was seen as a means of restricting the "contagion" of disabilities. "Eugenics" derives from a Greek word for "well born," and stands for the "science of improving the stock."

One of the chief engineers of IQ testing, Lewis Terman, expressed fears in 1924 that the "stock of gifted children" was waning. He compared with alarm the low fecundity of Harvard graduates with the high fecundity of southern Italians.

Eugenics proponents sought to encourage "fit" people (which tended to equate to the "well-to-do") to have children, and to prevent the "unfit" (insane, epileptic, alcoholic, poor, criminal, sexually perverse, drug-addicted, feebleminded) from having any. There were large efforts to gather data on communities, especially about people considered to be "social and mental defectives."

During the high period of influence (1905-1935), proponents of eugenics promoted involuntary-sterilization laws and the Immigration Restriction Act of 1924. "By 1931 some thirty states had compulsory-sterilization laws on their books" aimed at the insane and "feebleminded." The latter included many recent immigrants and those who did poorly on IQ tests (due to illiteracy or to poor English language skills).

"By January 1935 some twenty thousand people in the United States had been forcibly sterilized, nearly half of them in California. Indeed, the California law was not repealed until 1980 and eugenic-sterilization laws are still on the books [in 1990] in about twenty states."

The intent of the Immigration Restriction Act of 1924 was to decrease the number of poor immigrants from southern and eastern Europe, and to favor people of British or north European descent.

In Germany the "racial hygiene" movement gradually incorporated anti-Semitism. It was established as an academic discipline in 1923. By 1933, most medical schools in Germany taught eugenics and racial hygiene.

Hubbard notes that medical scientists, not the Nazis, invented racial hygiene in Germany. Their intention was not punitive, but rather corrective in terms of the health of the population. Genetic health courts determined who should be sterilized. "By 1939 some four hundred thousand people had been sterilized." The health courts were separate from activity in the concentration camps. They did not seek sterilization on the basis of race. Still, 500 mixed-race children were sterilized.

Soon the sterilization laws incorporated racial criteria, and then severely mentally ill patients (including children) in state psychiatric hospitals, and then children with Down syndrome. Gradually, the program expanded to include older children and then healthy Jewish children. By 1941, 70,000 inmates of hospitals had been killed, using gas chambers disguised as showers, with crematoria, an innovation exported to extermination camps later.

Thus the sterilization and euthanasia programs initiated by scientists and physicians for the mentally ill and physically disabled set the stage for broader definitions of who was "undesirable" and "worthless."

Just as sterilization was introduced to prevent the propagation of categories of "undesirables," and euthanasia was adopted to eliminate them, selective abortion is a strategy for preventing the birth of a "defective" fetus. Prenatal testing has made it possible to detect the presence of certain severe inherited diseases such as Down syndrome, spina bifida (a spine that fails to close), and anencephaly (failure to develop a brain). Legalized abortion has made it possible to choose to terminate pregnancy.

Hubbard argues that there are many ambiguities surrounding the choice to abort or not. First is the determination whether a fatal condition warrants early termination.

Then, whether an inherited illness is truly going to produce a "life not worth living," and whether sooner or later in that life. There are economic considerations – the cost or "burden" of caring for a severely disabled child. The medical professionals can pressure parents one way or the other, projecting personal opinions and values. There is no such thing as an objective, informed choice. We see historically how thinking about the right to live can be corrupted by ideology and misuses of scientific and medical knowledge.

>Hubbard, R. (2010). Abortion and disability: Who should and should not inhabit the world? In L.J. Davis (Ed.), *The Disability Studies reader* (3rd Ed.) (pp. 107-119). New York: Routledge.

REPRODUCTIVE RIGHTS

The goals of the reproductive rights movement now are in collision with the disability rights movement. "The reproductive rights movement emphasizes the right to have an abortion; the disability rights movement, the right *not to have to have* an abortion."

Because of the stigma surrounding disabilities, women who are in wheelchairs, blind, deaf, scarred, missing limbs, or on crutches may find themselves pressured to forgo having children. General ignorance about disability leads the public to think that the quality of life for disabled people is inferior, that raising a disabled child is a burden, and that selective abortion is an opportunity to spare parents that burden.

Saxton's point is that "oppression is what's most disabling about disability." Our culture invalidates disabled bodies, denies their sexuality, and discourages parenthood. Selective abortion is seen as a means to "end suffering." Yet individuals having Down's syndrome, spina bifida, cystic fibrosis, and other conditions may not agree that their lives are not worth living.

Disability rights activists do not want to be aligned with the "right to life" movement either. Anti-abortion groups have not tended to include in their agenda the idea of increasing the resources for disabled people or parents of disabled children that would make life easier. "They have shown no interest in disabled people after they are born."

>Saxton, M. (2010). Disability rights and selective abortion. In L.J. Davis (Ed.), The Disability Studies reader (3rd Ed.) (pp. 120-132). New York: Routledge.

GENETICS

The study of genetics currently also reinforces the social stigma associated with disability. The human genome is treated as a fixed "Book of Life," and research is focused on locating "defective genes" and disease-transmitting genes, with the goal of eliminating disease and the effects of "bad genes." As with eugenics, persons with disabilities are cast as mistakes. The rationale for funding genetic research can include the argument that the public burden of disease is great and would be reduced if we were to prevent defects such as spina bifida (estimated to cost nearly $300,000 per lifetime of an affected infant).

Wilson argues that an apolitical approach is to view genes as widely varied, dynamic, and indeterminate, with their expression depending on interaction with other genes and with the biological and psychological environment of the human body. We need to dispense with "ideological baggage." It is challenging because a simpler and emotional view ("genes gone bad") is easier to grasp.

> Wilson, J.C. (2010). Disability and the human genome. In L.J. Davis (Ed.), *The Disability Studies reader* (3rd Ed.) (pp. 52-62). New York: Routledge.

ECONOMIC OPPRESSION

The status of people with disabilities has been framed until recently in terms of deviance and stigma. Recently, it is reframed in terms of society's structures, especially socio-economic structures, and oppression.

The socio-cultural view characterizes persons with disabilities as outcasts – the Other. The roots of this status are seen as psychological processes, such as fear and pity. "The attitudes are almost universally pejorative. They hold that people with disabilities are pitiful and that disability itself is abnormal."

A political-economic view is that people with disabilities are an "underclass," considered a "surplus population" and relegated to poverty. The dynamics of power and control can be seen in the tracking of students in school. "Students with disabilities, as soon as their disability is recognized by school officials, are placed on a separate track. They are immediately labeled by authorized (credentialed) professionals (who never themselves have experienced these labels) as ED, ED EMH, and so on. The meaning and definition of all the labels differ, but they all signify inferiority on their face. ... Students are constantly told what they can do and what they cannot do from the very date of their labeling."

"Special education ... has been transformed from a way to increase the probability that students with disabilities will get some kind of an education into a badge of inferiority and a rule-bound, bureaucratic process of separating and then warehousing millions of young people." Students are told they cannot become teachers because they use wheelchairs, and discouraged from other "unrealistic vocations." Deaf students are given only hearing teachers so that they will learn to read lips. Teachers in segregated schools wear white lab coats to symbolize their role as medical helpers.

The hegemony (legitimized authority) and oppression is maintained with the help of the mass media. The media, like the state and the doctor, serve as authority figures. Mass media depictions transmit what is permissible – independence, family, sexuality. This includes the image of the "pitiful cripple" on telethons and the "helpless and angry cripple" in television shows. As a result, the person with disabilities is dehumanized and alienated.

> Charlton, J. (2010). The dimensions of disability oppression. In L.J. Davis (Ed.), *The Disability Studies reader* (3rd Ed.) (pp. 147-159). New York: Routledge.

MYTHS ABOUT THE PERFECT BODY

"Many people consider providing resources for disabled people a form of charity, superogatory in part because the disabled are perceived as unproductive members of society. Yet most disabled people are placed in a double-bind: they have access to inadequate resources because they are unemployed or underemployed, and they are unemployed or underemployed because they lack the resources that would enable them to make their full contribution to society."

"Often governments and charity organizations will spend far more money to keep disabled people in institutions… than they will spend to enable the same people to live independently and productively."

"Disability is also frequently regarded as a personal or family problem rather than a matter of social responsibility…. Many factors contribute to determining whether providing a particular resource is regarded as a social or a personal (or family) responsibility. One such factor is whether the majority can identify with people who need the resource."

"Many, perhaps most, able-bodied people do not want to know about suffering caused by the body…. Suffering caused by the body, and the inability to control the body, are despised, pitied, and above all, feared."

"The disabled are constant reminders to the able-bodied of the negative body—of what the able-bodied are trying to avoid, forget and ignore."

Among our cultural myths are that health is a virtue, and that the body can be controlled. The main purpose of medicine is to control the body. "The disabled often symbolize failure to control the body and the failure of science and medicine to protect us all."

"Dependence on the help of others is humiliating in a society which prizes independence."

> Wendell, S. (2010). Toward a feminist theory of disability. In L.J. Davis (Ed.), *The Disability Studies reader* (3rd Ed.) (pp. 336-352). New York: Routledge.

DEFINING DEAFNESS: SIGN LANGUAGE VERSUS ORAL ENGLISH

"The meaning of deafness changed during the course of the nineteenth century for educators of the deaf, and the kind of education deaf people received changed along with it." Early in the nineteenth century, deafness was considered an affliction whose worst effect was to isolate deaf people from learning the gospel and Christian truth. This concern was preeminent until the 1860s. Gradually, however, the concern shifted from worry about salvation to a worry about the tragedy of excluding deaf people from English-speaking society.

The earliest schools for deaf students were established by evangelical Protestant reformers concerned about saving souls. They relied on sign language in order to provide a Christian education. This had the effect of creating community among deaf people that was linguistically and culturally separate. The students lived in communal settings as a distinctive community.

After the 1860s, however, another movement acted on the fear that deaf people were forming a separate community. It emphasized learning to speak English and communicating with non-deaf English speakers. This group succeeded in controlling the schools, to the point that more than 80% of deaf people were taught entirely without sign language through the 1970s. The movement was called "oralists."

Deaf adults strenuously opposed the elimination of sign language. Forcing oral-or-nothing learning resulted in poor education, because it cut deaf students off from learning until they could grasp oral methods. With sign language as a mediating form of communication, they were able to learn faster. However, deaf people did not control schooling. Strong oralists, including the prominent Alexander Graham Bell, were motivated by eugenics and the belief that deafness was hereditary, and a fear that an isolated and cohesive deaf community would intermarry and propagate, spreading more deafness. It was a time of fear for the rise of immigrant communities and ethnic social enclaves, diluting the social order. Bell spoke of a "great calamity" from the high rate of intermarriage among deaf people.

The "manualists," or proponents of the use of sign language struggled for control over education. A new journal called *American Annals of the Deaf and Dumb* was published after 1847 and helped define the identity of deaf people as a community with a history. The journal published accounts of deaf people who were deprived of education, especially moral and religious knowledge – "the light of the divine truth." They "lived in darkness" like heathens or animals. The metaphor of "a silent exile on this earth" captures the worry.

The linguistic difference posed by sign language was associated with "being foreign." The oralists emphasized the image of an "insular, inbred, and proliferating death community with its own 'foreign' language and culture."

"The metaphors of deafness – of isolation and foreignness, of animality, of darkness and silence—are projections reflecting the needs and standards of the dominant culture, not the experiences of most deaf people."

Oralists faced a demise in the 1970s as deaf people organized, as a beleaguered minority. Support for sign language was expressed in lobbying to legislatures and school boards.

"Manualists and oralists had paternalism in common.... Both groups saw deafness through their own biases. ... Both used similar clusters of metaphors to forge images of deaf people as fundamentally flawed, incomplete, isolated, and dependent. And both used that imagery to justify not only the methods of education, but also the inherent authority of the hearing over people who were deaf. Still, deaf people sided with the manualists." Sign language gave deaf people a means to communicate among themselves and create their own identity and meaning. They would not give that up to please the oralists whose main value was assimilation, and not deaf identity and self-determination.

Baynton, Douglas (2006). A silent exile on this earth. In L.J. Davis (Ed.), *The Disability Studies reader* (2nd Ed.) (pp. 33-48). New York: Routledge.

TWO DEAF SUBCULTURES

The division between oralists and manualists is reflected in the use of conventions: "deaf" versus "Deaf." These words are codes for two sides of the controversy.

There is a fierce division among deaf people over the issue of whether they should learn to "pass" as people with hearing, for example learning to read lips, or, whether they are fine as members of a subculture with its own linguistic form, signing with the hands. The first group considers deafness as a disability. The latter, using the label "Deaf," considers itself a linguistic minority.

Each social construction has its historical roots and organizations advancing the viewpoint, in order to influence the choices of parents of deaf children, and the investment in educational and support resources. Each is the foundation of a "troubled-persons industry" or professionals who "owe their livelihood to deafness problems."

The first group – viewing deafness as a personal tragedy to be fixed – supports keeping deaf children in mainstream schools. Hearing teachers help the child and the family cope with a handicap, socializing the child to learn to lip read and to use hearing aids or cochlear implants, if possible, to correct the impairment. The goal is equal participation in society by people with deafness and requires medical strategies and rehabilitation.

The second group does not view deafness as a disability. "Deaf people are not deficient within their own community." "Deafness is a difference, not a deficiency." Just as Blacks would refuse operations to change their skin color and eliminate what sets them apart, more than 8 out of 10 Deaf adults would decline an implant operation and don't consider themselves handicapped. Society should accept sign language among linguistic options and use it in schools, like Spanish. Feelings for sign language and the culture are so strong that "Deaf people marry Deaf people 90 percent of the time in the U.S." The best method for transmitting the language and culture is through segregated schools, because hearing parents cannot pass on the Deaf language and culture to deaf children.

The critique against the first group is that it is premised in a "disability model" - that hearing-impaired people are deficient and need many special services to learn to function in "normal" society. The negative identity "colonizes" individuals and results in their internalizing a self-image of deficiency and dependence. The cochlear-implant industry is aggressively promoting cochlear implants in children although only one in ten deaf children can benefit. The needs of the related "troubled-persons industries" are driving policy, for example, advocating legislation that requires early detection and mandatory, publicly-funded services. Children learning in mainstream schools through lip reading may struggle to communicate and to perform. Deaf adults are mostly excluded from the ranks of professionals serving deaf children taught along this path.

The critique against the second group is that it isolates Deaf people from mainstream education and social assimilation, making them "foreigners." Proponents emphasize that the segregation is chosen. But advocates within the disability rights movement protest segregated institutions, expressing abhorrence due to the historical marginalization of persons with disabilities, the implication of being patronized (or "colonized"), and being "served" under the control of able-bodied professionals and vested industries.

"Both pay the price of social stigma. Both struggle with the troubled-persons industries for control of their destiny." Both benefit from voice-to-text and text-to-voice technologies that can mediate communication between non-hearing and hearing-only people.

However, "people who have little familiarity with deafness find the disability construction self-evident and the minority construction elusive." It is hard to imagine someone who becomes deaf later in life joining the Deaf community, separating from the English-speaking majority for a social life. The infrastructure supporting the interests of deaf individuals – teacher training programs and those who accredit them, university research facilities, professional conferences, specialized journals, medical and support service providers – is dominated by the "deafness as a disability" view. Its proponents are most established and most accessible to the media and to law and policy makers.

> Lane, H. (2010). Construction of deafness. In L.J. Davis (Ed.), *The Disability Studies reader* (3rd Ed.) (pp. 77-93). New York: Routledge.

IMPACT OF COCHLEAR IMPLANTS

The availability and perceived success of cochlear implants for people who are deaf has caused some consternation in the manualist community. Cochlear implants at any age make it possible for deaf people to hear enough to "cross over" from relying on hand gestures to lip reading, and making sounds in response. If the individual or their family is intensely vested in "manualism" and cultural identity as a deaf person, this can provoke fierce family dynamics. The question is whether a deaf child should be "repaired" or left in a natural condition, respecting a cultural identity.

> Communication from Jean Sando, December, 2010. More information can be found searching "cochlear implant controversy."

MENTAL RETARDATION

Mental retardation emerged as a social problem in the second quarter of the 19th Century. It has been viewed variously since that time as "a disorder of the senses, a moral flaw, a medical disease, a mental deficiency, a menace to the social fabric, and finally as mental retardation." Its social construction varies with the interest in *science* versus interest in *care* versus interest in *social control*.

In the 1840s mental retardation was a family and a local problem that shifted to being a social problem of the state. Custodial facilities arose initially for the care of mentally retarded people, but the interest of social control soon entered into justifications for institutions. With Edward Seguin came the exploration of educating mentally retarded people, with an assumption that they could be productive, although in institutional settings.

The rise of professional administrators and social welfare agents possibly contributed to the era of control, driven by an interest in legitimizing and solidifying their role and livelihood. Trent suggests that the link of care with social control went beyond the interests of their clients, when administrators supported castration and sterilization during the time of eugenics. At the time of the Great Depression in particular, sterilization made it possible to return inmates to the community "safely."

In the early 20th Century, mental retardation was reconstructed as a menace. The period saw the development of intelligence tests to calibrate mental fitness, eugenics (the notion that we needed to improve the human species by controlling reproduction), and anti-immigrant movements (keeping out people with undesirable impairments).

After World War II, abuse and neglect was exposed in state schools. Parents and advocates organized. The National Association for Retarded Children was founded in the 1950s. By the 1970s, institutions started to be closed or shut down. This was due to the convergence of a push for civil rights and independent living within community settings, and the states' interest in reducing costs.

Edward Seguin developed his system of education in France. He published several influential works in French and later in English after immigrating to the United States. He was inherently an advocate, seeking to redeem "young idiots" from squalor and humiliation, turning them into proper and working citizens in society. The burning question that caught the attention of social reformers in America was, can deficiencies of human intelligence be reclaimed? Schools for deaf, blind, and "dumb" students were finding success. But could idiocy be cured, or corrected? Seguin introduced the idea of education and training to the American system.

Seguin addressed only "young idiots, who were free from epilepsy, paralysis, and insanity," and who were not "imbeciles." He held little hope for helping those he considered imbeciles. He thought American asylums were treating idiots like children, when they could be put to work.

Late in his life he saw the growth and growing size of institutions and a gradual compromise in efforts to educate and train.

Many of Seguin's techniques and theoretical foundations are still available and practiced, although there have been improvements. Although he disagreed with the trend toward institutionalization, his ideas facilitated it, as superintendents used his philosophy and his name to justify the growth of state residential facilities.

The transition from state institutions to community life has not been completely positive. While abuses in institutions were corrected, the infrastructure for support in the communities was not there when residents came out. People lost services. Some were re-institutionalized in various non-profit and for-profit organizations, or jails and prisons. There were many negative unintended consequences to flooding communities with mentally retarded individuals.

A significant issue for persons with intellectual disabilities is their economic vulnerability. People who were capable of work were sequestered for nearly a century. They were incarcerated, seen as a burden to their parents and the community and as a menace to society. During periods of economic prosperity (1920s) or need (World War II), the "sterilized morons" were welcomed back out to work. Economic "worth" is a persistent question, especially in a society that has a premium on productivity and profit.

In the 1970s, federal courts declared unpaid or underpaid inmate labor to be involuntary servitude, and illegal. This resulted in a flux toward new urban training centers.

> Trent, J. (1995). *Inventing the feeble mind: A history of mental retardation in the United States*. Berkeley: University of California Press.

BIOETHICS

The biggest questions in bioethics are about the right to be born, the right to die, and the right to treatment. The answers are deeply felt and rarely clear-cut. There is a disability rights perspective on each of them, particularly when the answer is tied to assumptions about the quality of life for a person with a particular impairment.

Historically, persons with disabilities have been treated as less-than-human and devalued. During World War II in Germany, and later in the United States, cognitively disabled inmates of institutions were used as the subjects of medical research without their consent. Individuals and organizations such as the National Federation of the Blind during the 1960s and 1970s protested the paternalism of "caring" professionals and insisted on representation on boards of services agencies that made decisions about treatment, to protect their interests. The question is especially poignant when a patient's life can be sustained using technology such as mechanical respiration or tube feeding.

The Western bioethics establishment agrees with the disability rights movement in its commitment to patient rights, skepticism about professional power over medical decisions, and the need for consumer/patient protection.

Now that we can save premature babies, save more wounded soldiers or those injured in car accidents, and stroke victims, we increasingly have to address the question of **whether the sanctity of life is important at any cost, in any state of impairment**. We *can* save lives, but *should* they be saved? Bioethicists say that the quality of life after treatment should be a factor in medical decision making. The disability rights movement says that usually decisions about quality of life with impairment tend to be biased and misinformed. People making medical decisions are often not aware that people with certain disabilities can and do lead satisfying lives, and prefer to stay alive.

Newborns with impairments. Should an infant born with Down syndrome, spina bifida, a severe bowel obstruction, or breathing problems, be treated for related problems, when the chances for survival are low, and the quality of life after treatment is extremely limited? Physicians and lawyers have debated when parents' wishes are pre-eminent, and when parents' wishes, for example, to withhold treatment, are overruled in the interest of the infant. There are many cases of law debating and settling the rights to life of infants with disabling conditions. Disability rights advocates argue that denying treatment represents discrimination against people with disabilities. They note that parents fear having the child and don't understand the potential for a satisfying life, and therefore give in to pressure to withhold treatment. In 2000, most infants with Down syndrome, spina bifida, and prematurity received medically indicated treatments. In later life cases, adults with Down syndrome have been denied organ transplants or kidney dialysis based on their impairment.

Prenatal testing and selective abortion. In the 1990s the advent of prenatal testing made it possible to detect the presence of certain impairments at a point where abortion could be elected, legally. Research shows that most people who seek testing plan to abort if they learn of a disability. A majority of geneticists who were surveyed believe that the general health and vigor of the population is improved by limiting the birth of severely impaired infants. Society has over time regarded disability as undesirable and to be avoided. Some parents even feel strongly that it is wrong to give birth to an infant who will suffer significantly and have significantly reduced life options; it is damaging to the family; it is costly to society. However, prenatal testing has made it possible to void the birth of a child whose only flaw is the wrong gender. Disability rights advocates maintain that selective abortion is biased, misused, and based on misinformation about quality of life with a disability.

Sustaining life with a disability. Both bioethicists and disability advocates hold that people should choose their own treatments, deciding whether their quality of life after treatment is worthwhile to them. But disability advocates point out that persons with disabilities are often pressured to decline treatment, even by their families, due to the perception that their quality of life is too poor.

The right to die. Similarly, there is fierce opposition to the prospect of voluntarily ending life. Some individuals with incurable and progressively worsening illnesses such as cerebral palsy or ALS, or spinal cord injury with no hope for rehabilitation, can live for decades with assistive technologies and the help of caretakers, but choose not to. Where physician-assisted suicide is not legal, they starve themselves or arrange for unauthorized over-medication or poison. Again, disability activists claim that the decision is not usually informed by the full range of options available to the patient, and, they blame society and the lack of supports for the patient's hopelessness. They are campaigning for better representation on hospital ethics committees and for better consideration of ways to improve the quality of life for the patient. The organization Not Dead Yet was formed in the 1990s around the issue of physician-assisted suicide. Their efforts contributed to a Supreme Court ruling against the right to assistance in dying, recognizing negative stereotypes , societal indifference, and a cost-saving mentality underlying decisions particularly made by or for persons with severe disabilities and terminal illness.

Right to accommodation and treatment as social justice. If we view disabilities as a manifestation of normal variation in the conditions of the human body, and we agree that all members of society need to be incorporated and encouraged, then we must conclude that society has an obligation to make accommodations that enable participation and life, including medical treatment. It is a controversial and political decision to invest in changes needed by less than one-fifth of the population. (We use "politics" here to mean the process of deciding who gets what from collective resources.)   Medical care "at any cost" for all is debated. Bioethics is now informed and influenced by the perspective of persons with disabilities, for example, articulated in "The Right To Live and To Be Different" by the Disabled People's International in 2000.

> Asch, A. (2001). Disability, bioethics, and human rights. In G. Albrecht, K. Seelman & M. Bury (Eds.), *Handbook of Disability Studies* (pp. 297-326). Thousand Oaks, CA: Sage.

HISTORY OF PSYCHIATRY

Psychiatry emerged at the end of the 18th Century. "People of villages and small towns had a horror of those who were different, an authoritarian intolerance of behavior that did not conform to rigidly drawn norms. …. Those who were forced by disorders of mind and mood to be different, to deviate from any of these rhythms, were dealt with in the most brutal and unfeeling manner."

Family, not the community, had to deal with them. Care was a family affair up until the 19th Century. As more asylums were introduced in the 1870s in Europe, a Swiss census found one-fifth of the mental patients under restraint at home, in unheated rooms and stables, locked up. Having madness was shameful.

There had been asylums since the Middle Ages. They had solely custodial functions. In American colonies, confinement of some sort for mental illness was evident. "Thus on both sides of the Atlantic, the history of psychiatry began as the history of the custodial asylum, institutions to confine raging individuals who were dangerous to themselves and a nuisance to others."

The notion that the institutions themselves could be curative changed at the end of the 18th Century. Confinement would make the patient better. "A new therapeutic optimism engulfed the world of medicine in the second half of the 18th century, an optimism that psychiatry shared." William Battie, a medical officer who founded an asylum in 1751 wrote *Treatise on Madness*, which specifically argued for the virtues of the asylum. He recommended an isolation cure, with no visits from friends. In 1794, Vincenzio Chiarugi published *On Insanity*, in which he made the case that asylums were not merely to segregate mental patients but to heal them. There were observations that psychiatric patients could develop their "faculties of reason" and had intervals of lucidity.

There arose the idea of the asylum as a therapeutic community – patients and physicians living in the psychiatric setting. The purpose of isolation was to divert patients from unhealthy passions and patterns. "Given the scarcity of doctors interested in insanity, it made much more sense to concentrate a few available doctors in institutions."

There were two kinds of institutions: for incurables and for the curable.

Two aspects of life in an asylum were therapeutic: the setting itself with orderly routines and communal spirit, and the doctor-patient relationship. The relationship with the doctor was called "moral therapy." The setting was not to be a "madhouse." Calming was important, as was order and structure – a kind of rest home. "Orderly life is restorative."

An important break from the past in late-eighteenth century was physicians started using techniques that were neither giving of medication nor physical procedures. This was the advent of psychotherapy, the formal use of the doctor-patient relationship to restore patients.

"Minor psychiatric illnesses fell heavily to the lot of spa doctors, in Europe." This included anxiety, neurotic depression, obsessive-compulsive behavior, "nervous illness," "psychoneurotic" disorders, hysteria, and hypochondria. Spas were visited by middle and upper classes for illnesses with no organic cause. In London, the society doctors were "nerve doctors." "Society nerve doctors arose during the eighteenth century in every country, outfitted with such diagnoses as hysteria, hypochondria, and spleen." They treated fatigue, pain, a sense of dullness, sadness, melancholy, and discouragement.

Doctors were known to keep their practices separate – treating nerves versus madness.

"Psychiatry has always been torn between two visions of mental illness. One vision stresses the neurosciences, with their interest in brain chemistry, brain anatomy, and medication, seeing the origin of the psychic distress in the biology of the cerebral cortex. The other vision stresses the psych-social side of patients' lives, attributing their symptoms to social problems or past personal stresses to which people may adjust imperfectly..... The neuroscience version is usually called biological psychiatry; the social-stress version makes great virtue of the bio-psychosocial model of illness."

At the beginning, the biological version was predominant. Psychiatry was neurology. "Psychiatrists of the founding generation also anticipated later biological psychiatry with their emphasis on heredity. ... they observed the recurrence of melancholia and suicide within families."

> Shorter, E. (1977). A history of psychiatry: From the era of the asylum to the age of Prozac. New York: John Wiley & Sons. Esp. Chap 1: The Birth of Psychiatry, pp. 1-32)

MODERN MENTAL ILLNESS

At the end of the twentieth century, psychiatry was science-driven, consistent with the rest of medicine. But it was enmeshed in popular values, corporate cultures, and "scientism" or pseudo-science. The focus on biology and neuroscience continued in the treatments of serious mental illness. However, society was increasingly concerned with vaguer disorders such as anxiety, stress, and neurotic tendencies. These disorders were not as clearly inherited, nor so severe that the patients had to be put into an asylum. As Shorter puts it, the "boundaries between pathology and eccentricity" are vague, and psychiatry drifted, and even lost its way, in the vagueness.

At the end of the twentieth century, people "psychologized" distress. Personal issues were more likely to be brought to a psychologist rather than a neurologist. Medicine was not seen as the answer. "Psychiatry, an arm of medicine, lost out to nonmedical forms of counseling such as psychology and social work." Postmodern distress flourished, with millions of Americans seeking help for mental problems. Psychotherapy passed from "an exotic procedure performed by neurologists to a virtual national pastime."

Clearly the threshold of what people defined as illness dropped; people were ready to admit dis-ease in the form of mental problems. Psychiatry itself helped in lowering the threshold. There was also a tendency to seek therapy for stress and life's problems. Therapy for personal distress "flooded" beyond psychiatry into the world of psychologists, psychiatric social workers, and counselors – "mental health professionals."

Psychiatrists have a self-interest in pathologizing human behavior. An example of this is in the discovery of "attention deficit disorder with hyperactivity" or ADHD, in 1980. It was found to be most prevalent among boys, who were exasperating, restless, and distracted in school. Appropriate treatment was medical therapy done by MDs, who could write prescriptions for Ritalin.

Similarly, Post Traumatic Stress Disorder, which originally was a label used for the trauma of combat that lingered among veterans, came to be applied to anxieties of children and others encountering trauma, even in the form of scary movies.

Likewise the boundaries of what is considered depression have expanded. In 1991, for example, "Mental Illness Awareness Screening Day" was introduced, with encouragement that family doctors refer potential patients to psychiatrists. Now, "depression has become the single most common disorder seen in psychiatric practice, accounting for more than one quarter of all patient visits."

"Personality disorders have become a whole sandbox for empire building." New illnesses appear, such as "antisocial personality disorder," "multiple personality disorder," and "borderline schizophrenia." The patient base is increasing accordingly. Psychiatrists had gone from focusing on psychotic patients, to neurotics, to people who had not normally been seen by medical practitioners at all. The focus shifted "from disease to unhappiness."

Psychiatrists were struggling to hold "market share" against nonmedical competitors. Insurance agencies of course resisted the trend toward more conditions that represented "billable psychiatric illness." Meanwhile the public clamored for psychotherapy. Social workers began to shift from social services to psychotherapy after World War I. The number of psychiatric or "clinical" social workers rose from 2,000 in 1945 to 55,000 in 1985, exceeding the numbers of psychiatrists. Their main client base was "white, middle class, 20-40-year-olds who are unhappy, unfulfilled, and unsatisfied. ... exactly the client base of post-1970s psychiatry."

Carl Rogers' work around 1950 jump-started psychology into a move from testing to psychotherapy. His approach was characterized as "humanistic" and "client-centered," and did not require complicated training as was the case with Freudian or Jungian analysis.

Psychiatrists rebelled but lost out. The American Psychiatric Association lobbied Congress to keep psychologists from prescribing drugs. By the 1990s, psychotherapy was a non-medical service. Even trained psychiatrists gravitated to the more lucrative business of psychoneurosis.

The ability of psychiatry to maintain its scientific foundation was challenged by the fact that psychiatrists did not know the causes of most conditions, unlike medicine in general. Conditions are classified based on symptoms, rather than causes. "This was where the rest of medicine was in the nineteenth century." Scientific credibility was further strained by the fact that conditions were diagnosed differently between different countries. Schizophrenia, for example, was fashionable among Americans. International differences in diagnosis were embarrassing, and unscientific. A large study in 1969 comparing diagnostic practice between the United States and the United Kingdom found them badly out of sync.

American medicine adopted a national standard for nomenclature of disease in the 1920s. The American Psychiatric Association contributed the psychiatric part. Until World War II, the naming system was devised for patients in public asylums with major mental illnesses. After the War, in 1952, however, the first of a series called Diagnostic and

Statistical Manual of Mental Disorders was developed, called DSM-I for short. DSM-II appeared in 1968. The standard expresses the dominant philosophy with each edition. For example, in DSM-II, homosexuality is included as a disorder, and in DSM-III (published in 1980) it is not. The standard improved consistency across clinics nationally. The DSM-IV was published in 1994. There were ideological lobbies for certain definitions. For example, Vietnam veterans held a campaign for the recognition of post-traumatic stress syndrome in DSM-III.

The focus on psychoanalysis declined with each evolution of the DSM series. The term "neurosis" was dropped. Competing psychotherapies proliferated into a hundred or more, and many dubious therapies were considered valid, without a scientific basis, such as "therapeutic touching." There were few statistical studies evaluating their effectiveness. Medical credentials were not required for many, and the public did not insist on them. Clinics for eating disorders, drug addiction, sexual disorders, and mental health competed for clients based on patient testimonials and unsubstantiated claims. The boundaries between medical treatment and "the human potential movement" eroded. Even psychiatrists pointed out that the effectiveness of intensive psychotherapy had never been established by means of rigorous clinical trials, and controlled trials were the hallmark of scientific medicine. A few studies that were initiated did not succeed in proving that psychoanalysis was any more effective than no treatment, or eclectic therapies.

The availability of new drugs made diagnosis more practically oriented, and more reliable, as psychiatrists focused on symptoms that indicated the prescription of certain drugs. Rather than offer in-depth psychoanalysis over a long period of time, the solution was "symptom relief," with quick results.

"By 1970, one woman in five and one man in thirteen was using minor tranquilizers and sedatives." A milestone in drug therapy was the development of Prozac by the Eli Lilly Company in 1990. Prozac was an anti-depressive. At the time, a study found that 10% of all Americans had depressive episodes, and 5% would have episodes of anxiety. Prozac, Valium, and new tranquilizers relieved these symptoms, with relatively few side effects. Pharmacists ran out of supplies because there was such great demand for the "happiness" drugs. "The share of psychiatric patients receiving prescriptions increased from a quarter of all office visits in 1975 to fully one-half by 1990." Psychiatry became a specialty that mainly provided medication.

The pharmacology industry flourished accordingly. New drugs were positioned for new disorders identified in the DSM. Clinical trials established appropriate prescription, and scientific validity. Manipulation of definitions of conditions, and diagnosis, was inevitable in finding the right market. Another well-known example of drug companies and their influence on psychiatric practice was the introduction of selective serotonin reuptake inhibitors (SSRIs) for the control of mood and drive. Prozac, less than three years after its appearance, became the number one drug prescribed by psychiatrists, for depression. "Millions of people … craved the new compound."

Another effect of popular drugs was that psychiatric symptoms lost their stigma. People had "stress," which could be treated. They were not mentally ill, or insane, nor moral failures. Advocacy groups played down the fear of mental illness and the feeling that the mentally ill needed to be or deserved to be isolated. "The face of madness has been completely changed."

"In two hundred years' time, psychiatrists had progressed from being the healers of the therapeutic asylum to serving as gatekeepers for Prozac. Psychiatric illness had passed from a feared sign of bad blood—a genetic curse—to an easily treatable condition." The strength of psychiatry as a profession was in its proprietary knowledge of the use of drugs. Many disorders that were medicalized were shifted to the purview of specialists such as internists, pediatricians, neurologists. However, psychiatry as a specialty still retains its psychotherapeutic emphasis on the doctor-patient relationship, which is in contrast to the treatment process as practiced by other medical specialists. Psychiatrists have the asset of authority of being a physician over psychologists and social workers, and the asset of a psychotherapeutic relationship with the patient over other physicians.

> Shorter, E. (1977). A history of psychiatry: From the era of the asylum to the age of Prozac. New York: John Wiley & Sons. Esp. Chap 8: From Freud to Prozac (pp. 288-327)

Special Education

Education policy in America expresses democratic values, that all children should be included. –L. Barton & F. Armstrong

FEDERALLY MANDATED

All public schools in the U.S. are required to offer a free and appropriate education to children with disabilities. The services called Special Education are guided by the regulations in the Individuals with Disabilities Education Improvement Act of 2004 (IDEIA).

Special education teacher teams assess the student and prepare an annual Individualized Education Plan, which spells out what services and assistance the child needs. The target school setting is as close as possible to the setting provided to children without disabilities.

Since the program is federally funded, there is much government support in carrying out programs consistent with the regulations. Accommodations and modifications that are suggested for students in every category under the IDEIA are also well documented for the benefit of teachers by special projects (usually funded by the government), such as Project Ideal.

U.S. Department of Education, Office of Special Education Programs (OSEP) IDEA website. http://idea.ed.gov/

Texas Council for Developmental Disabilities, Project IDEAL. Disability categories. Downloaded from http://www.projectidealonline.org/overview.php on May 17, 2010

STATISTICS

In 2007-08, about 13 percent of public school enrollment received special education services. Of those who received them, 39% received them for learning disabilities and 22% for speech or language impairments. Most of the students (80%) spent their school day in general classes.

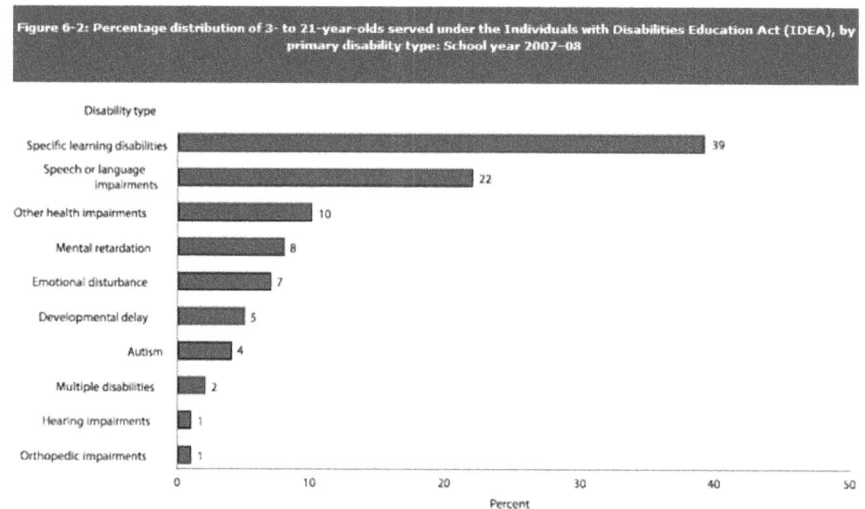

Aud, S., Hussar, W., Planty, M., Snyder, T., Bianco, K., Fox, M., Frohlich, L., Kemp, J., Drake, L. (2010). *The Condition of Education 2010* (NCES 2010-028). National Center for Education Statistics, Institute of Education Sciences, U.S. Department of Education. Washington, DC.

INTERNATIONAL VALUE ON INCLUSION

Access to formal education in any society Is a means of access to employment and socioeconomic status. It is a political issue of who is included in public systems, and in what roles. Access to education can reinforce inequalities, overtly or covertly. The child's social capital, in the form of the parents' status, knowledge and resources, can determine the level of access to educational opportunities.

There are international measures for the percentage of school children classified as disabled. One source is the study *Integrating Students with Special Needs into Mainstream Schools* by the Organization for Economic Cooperation and Development in 1995. There are problems with international comparisons, for example, different ways of defining disability and the quality of education provided.

Education policy in America expresses democratic values, that all children should be included. The UN communicates the value as well.

Barton, L. & Armstrong, F. (2001). Cross-cultural issues and dilemmas. In G. Albrecht, K. Seelman & M. Bury (Eds.), *Handbook of Disability Studies* (pp. 693-710). Thousand Oaks, CA: Sage.

ORIGINS OF SPECIAL EDUCATION

Public school systems evolved out of reforms in the late 19th century. There were massive upheavals due to urbanization, industrialization, and immigration. Children were working in bad conditions. Rates of poverty and crime were high. States claimed responsibility over schools and over the lives of children. Massachusetts led the way: first state Board of Education in 1837, and nation's first true compulsory education law in 1853. By 1900, most states had done the same. Schools were charged to assume a greater role as a social service and as an acculturation agency.

There was growing apprehension about the growing presence of persons with disabilities, especially those with "mental deficiency." Accordingly, there was growing interest in institutionalizing, educating, treating, and even curing persons with disabilities. "The perceived need for greater control over individuals and social groups—especially of poor and/or immigrant populations—grew."

European educators had argued for special educational settings that emphasized positive, individualized attention – a "child centered education." This idea migrated to the U.S. One-on-one instruction was already a hallmark of education of deaf and blind children. The educator Eduoard Seguin brought his 'physiological method' for teaching individual children with severe mental disabilities to the United States. It became the cornerstone of early formal education efforts in this nation's first institutions for the mentally disabled.

The Boston School Committee changed its intermediate schools into "ungraded classes" which soon became "dumping grounds" for students who were struggling or misbehaved. It was a solution to "the harsh reality of widely divergent cultures, backgrounds, needs, abilities, and interests among its students."

"In 1869, [Boston] established a public day school for deaf students. In 1895, Boston started a Parental School for truants and other transgressors, which became the Disciplinary Day School in 1915. In 1899, the Boston public schools opened its first class for students identified as 'mentally deficient.' Within the next fifteen years, specialized classes and programs for children with chronic illnesses, vision impairments, speech disorders, giftedness, and low English proficiency were created. … By the 1920s, special education stood as an established aspect of public schools in the city, with over 5 percent of children enrolled in a designated specialized setting."

By the first decade of the twentieth century, Chicago, New York, Cleveland, Baltimore, Philadelphia, and Los Angeles had taken similar approaches. "By the 1920s, 'special classes' for children with mental retardation were standard in most large school systems and in some smaller ones. The National Education Association (NEA) formed a Department of Special Education shortly after 1900. … By 1930 in the United States, special education in urban public schools had become a standard feature of public education. "

It was mostly an urban phenomenon. Rural schools lacked teachers who could provide special education.

One motivation for public services was to relieve the pressure on families to care for a disabled child, especially one with mental disability. But also, there was public concern about how much the home environment contributed to behavior and health disorders that became a public burden. Public officials recognized that placing mentally disabled persons in workhouses, almshouses, jails, and lunatic asylums did not serve best for education and treatment. Custodial care was not a good answer.

Residential institutions for deaf and blind students were true schools rather than custodial warehouses or pseudo-prisons. Day schools gradually appeared, due to lower costs, and skepticism about the propriety and effectiveness of residential settings.

The flagship settings for special education programs were classes for "feebleminded" or "mentally defective" children between the late 1910s and 1920s. Doctors helped place the children, separating "truants" or "juvenile delinquents" from those not likely to learn. Standardized intelligence tests were introduced in 1916 providing a 'scientific' approach to identifying mentally defective children. There were abuses, for example, reports of using the class to 'dump' non-conforming students or disliked ethnicities (Jews, Italians, African-Americans). Thus the classes could mix capable students (there by reason of ethnicity or a disease not affecting intelligence), psychopathic, and those having low intelligence. Intelligence testing improving on selection by reason of biases.

Special classes proved of such value that they quickly expanded, especially for children with mental disabilities, through the 1980s. Teaching special classes became a professional specialty. The work was particularly difficult, and the classes and students had a lower status. Parents resisted and refused placement of their children, refusing to believe their child was in any way limited, even though special instruction could improve the child's education. Teacher training varied between approaches for deaf, blind, or mentally disabled students. Speech improvement was added as a specialization. Professional journals helped solidify professional identity and standards.

Chronically ill children were also accommodated with a slower pace, cots for resting, and exposure to fresh air. Children with problems related to physical mobility were offered transportation, wheel chairs, crutches, or braces, and special desks and exercise equipment.

Large cities issued reports, sharing best practices and drawing attention to success stories. In the 1930s and 1940s, articles addressed issues and practices. An article by Goodwin Watson challenged the problem- or deficit-driven paradigm that had dominated special education and the social treatment of disability, expressing the view that disabled children were a "neglected resource" and we should find ways to take advantage of what they can offer, not focus on deficits. Later papers spoke of emphasizing respect rather than pity, cooperation rather than patronage, assimilation rather than segregation." We should judge children by their abilities, and not disabilities. Children should not be seen as liabilities. We need a broader concept of "normalcy." [These themes are echoed in the later disability rights movement.]

Gradually special education spread to nursery schools, with research findings that early interventions were effective. Similarly, there was expansion into high school, adding preparation for work and participation in society.

During World War II, persons with disabilities were called to fill in jobs formerly held by men who left for war. Returning veterans also changed the public perception of disability to be more positive and accepting.

The rise in parent-advocate associations and the disability rights movement raised awareness about disabilities and led to Federal legislation. The Education for All Handicapped Children Act of 1975 marked a turning point in efforts to support all children with disabilities and integrate them in schools and in society. Racial integration of schools paralleled integration of special education for children with disabilities.

Testing students for eligibility grew more sophisticated. "The link between poverty, minority status, and special education eligibility attracted considerable attention even before 1960."

Many residential schools were renamed "training schools" or "development centers" to improve their public image and emphasize their original mission. Still, they provided mostly custodial care, for children with more serious mental retardation, from all socioeconomic classes.

New categories of disability appeared: Samuel Kirk introduced the construct of "learning disabilities" in 1963. By the 1980s, learning disabilities were the single largest category of disability recognized under federal law. Identifying children with learning disabilities was more difficult and controversial than mental retardation. They often became apparent only after a student started to flounder in school. Parents were reluctant to label their child as disabled and have them assigned to special educational interventions. There were new guides on how to recognize learning disabilities. The demand for public school programs exceeded supply, and private schools were established just for this category of disability.

In addition, public laws recognized Traumatic Brain Injury, Autism, and Attention Deficit-Hyperactivity Disorder.

Entering the 21st Century, we do not question whether public schools should accommodate children with disabilities. The question is now how much and in what ways, and how much funding is available to accommodate a wide range of kinds of disabilities. Can all the needs be met? Can the legal obligation be met with the financial resources available? The United Cerebral Palsy Association prepared "A Bill of Rights for the Handicapped" that invokes the right to education "to the fullest extent to which [a child] is intellectually capable, provided through the regular channels of American education."

Just as our society is questioning the boundaries of medical intervention in health care, it is also questioning the boundaries of educational intervention in special education. For example, one critic cited $60,000 per year spent on a three-year-old with severe mental illness.

> Osgood, R. L. (2008). *The history of special education: A struggle for equality in American public schools*. Westport, Conn: Praeger.

CONTROVERSIES

There are a number of issues that persist in special education.

There is disagreement about who belongs in special education. "Determining who was handicapped and who needed special education has itself been a torturous process. Was it someone who needed aid to survive physically or economically? Or was it someone who had a learning disability, couldn't "get along" in school, failed to keep up to grade level, or scored low on an IQ test? From its inception, some have condemned special education for not being available to enough children, and some, especially parents of handicapped children, have demanded more as well as better programs. Yet others have condemned special education for too readily identifying children as handicapped, and too readily placing them in segregated special classes."

Special education was linked to studies of retardation and intelligence testing. Studies found 34% of all early elementary children were behind in their grade and overage for their classes. The reasons were unclear: illness, late entrance, irregular attendance? Retardation was associated with immigrants, truants, and the mentally deficient. Special schooling was motivated by humanitarian concerns, and also interests in controlling deviant behavior and the social threat it posed. "Special education would cut down truancy and neglect, and thereby reduce criminal behavior."

"Indeed, no argument associated with special education received greater attention in the first three decades of the twentieth-century than the fear that the unattended or uneducated feebleminded were the carriers of social malignancy." Testing found at least 2% of the school population mentally defective. Research into families confirmed that mental deficiency was a hereditary characteristic. "Feeblemindedness is a serious menace to the social, economic and moral welfare of the state. ... It is responsible for at least one fourth of the commitments to state penitentiaries & reform schools, for the majority of cases of chronic and semi-chronic pauperism, and for much of our alcoholism, prostitution and venereal disease." Case study of New Jersey showed a large reduction in the number of youth committed to state reformatories after special education was introduced. New Jersey special education classes were overwhelmingly populated by immigrant and behavior problem children.

A California survey found 1-4% of children "feebleminded" – consistently above 2%. "At least half should be institutionalized." "At least 1% should be segregated in residential custodial institutions, and preferably sterilized. Another 2.5 % belonged in special classes, and an additional 15% should be provided the kind of manually and vocationally oriented education that would prevent them from becoming burdens to the society." "Throughout the country, special education received its major impetus from the application of testing to the immigrant and the poor."

Special education has been associated with racism and cultural bias against immigrants. "From its origins, special education was tied to views of racial inferiority. Without the ethnic and racial antagonisms of the World War I years, special education would have received only the most minimal attention. … Racial biases made minorities the most likely candidates for placement in inadequate special education classes…. Public schools incorporated large numbers of nonwhite pupils into the schools while simultaneously segregating them within the schools [in California, circa 1947). Special education thus became disproportionately populated by nonwhites and foreign language children." There was criticism of racial and cultural bias in intelligence tests which were used extensively to assign students to special education. "In California, special education originated and remained a class and racially based system; it was not to change."

There was also the motivation of protecting "normal" students, and regular classroom teachers, from the disruptions of both "naughty" and "stupid" children. The state institutions could not accommodate all feebleminded children. "It was absolutely necessary to get the handicapped out of regular classrooms. …They were a trial to teachers." Teachers were enthusiastic about grouping students by ability.

The legislation mandating the provision of special education placed a new burden on public schools. There is resentment for the cost. The interest in providing child welfare was integrated with the educational agenda.

Special educators have to compete for adequate resources. During the Depression, these programs were cut first. "Special education has always remained an outsider, subject to second-class citizenship." "The financial costs of educating handicapped children were high—two and a half to four and a half times the cost of regular elementary school classes, depending on the handicap."

Much evidence showed, eventually, that the investment in special education paid off in reducing other social burdens such as the need for reformatories and prisons.

Ironically, special education also came to be seen as an entitlement and desirable benefit. By early 1970s, middle-class white parents of children with disabilities led the attack on their exclusion from the educational system. They demanded the right to have education of their handicapped children recognized as a public responsibility. "Children had a right to an adequate education." Instead of being a "dumping ground," special education became a civil right.

"These were the contexts of the emerging revolution in special education: an extraordinary expansion in the size and cost of special education; parents demanding access to and adequacy in special education; the spillover of the civil rights movement determined to prevent segregation, stigmatization, and de facto second-class citizenship through improper classification; and special educators and related professions willing to join parental lobbies on behalf of handicapped children."

> Lazerson, M. (1983). The origins of special education. In J.G. Chambers & W.T. Hartman (Eds.), *Special Education Policies: Their history, implementation, and finance (pp. 15-47)*. Philadelphia: Temple University Press.

CURRENT

Three cities have a reputation for excellence in inclusion of students with disabilities in regular classes: Madison, WI, Charlotte-Mecklenburg, NC, and Clark County, NV. It costs Madison $23,000 to educate a child with autism, versus $12,000 for a regular child. Fewer than 5% of disabled students are schooled separately [in 2010].

> A school district that takes the isolation out of autism. *New York Times* (August 2, 2010), A9.

Learning Disabilities

The cause of most intellectual disabilities is not known. – Centers for Disease Control

DEFINITIONS

There are several impairments associated with the brain.

"Intellectual disabilities" or "cognitive disabilities" used to be called **"mental retardation."** It is characterized by significant limitation in thinking and everyday skills. It usually originates before the age of 18. One measure is an IQ test, with a score less than 70/75. Causes include genes, prenatal environment (e.g. alcohol), a birth event (e.g., low oxygen), or a health problem (e.g., malnutrition, disease). It is also called **"developmental disability."** There is no known cure.

Autism Spectrum Disorder including **Asperger Syndrome** are classified as developmental disorders. They are the result of a neurological disorder that affects normal functioning of the brain and especially social interaction and communication. Symptoms usually appear between the ages of 2 and 6.

Attention-Deficit Hyperactivity Disorder (ADHD or AD/HD) is also a developmental disorder. A person having ADHD displays abnormal levels of inattention and/or hyperactivity. A child might be extremely impulsive and have difficulty with self-control.

"Learning disability" refers to difficulty learning specific skills such as reading, arithmetic, and reasoning. The child has normal or above average intelligence but his brain processes information differently. There is no known cure but there are skills that can be learned to manage the difficulty. Children with learning disabilities can be high achievers.

Mental illness is disease of the mind – a disruption of a person's normal cognitive, emotional, or behavioral functioning enough to reduce his ability to cope with ordinary life. It can be caused by disease, trauma, genes, or other factors. It is also called **emotional illness**. It does not imply low intelligence or learning difficulties. It can occur any time in the course of a lifetime. For example, Post Traumatic Stress can occur as the result of a traumatic event. Some mental illnesses may not manifest in early childhood but later (e.g., bipolar disorder, schizophrenia). Mental illness is treatable and can be cured or managed through medication or psychosocial treatment.

Clearly there are differences in severity within any of these categories. Historical accounts about the poor treatment of persons with disabilities are often referring to persons with extreme intellectual disabilities – the "idiot" or "feebleminded." For the purposes of assessment for special education, there is a distinction between "Intellectual Disabilities" and "Specific Learning Disabilities," which correlates with severity.

TRENDS

There is a surge in the number of students labeled learning disabled. In 1995, they comprised 46% of students in special education. The definition is still disputed. It may appear as "an imperfect ability to listen, think, speak, read, write, and spell or to do mathematical calculations." It may also include "a short attention span, impulsiveness, difficulty telling or understanding jokes, chronic tardiness and trouble reading maps." "Are such traits merely personality quirks?"

Some educators object to broad labeling. They think that underachieving or lazy students are claiming the disability. Is accommodation simply a matter of setting lower academic standards, especially at the college level?

The ambiguity and inconsistency in diagnosis shows up in the different rates of prevalence among states – 3% to 10% (Georgia and Massachusetts).

The most common learning disability is dyslexia, a difficulty reading. The brain's processing of phonemes, or sounds, is irregular. It is not considered curable. There is new evidence that suggests it may be inherited.

About 3% of students at the college level claim to have learning disabilities. Accommodations at the college level are controversial. First, there is the cost involved in making accommodations, which are required by law, in the form of student services (e.g., providing note takers, tutors, tape recorders, software). Critics say that there is a trend to treat any academic weakness as an incurable learning disability, and that academic standards are compromised. Proponents point out that the disabilities must be diagnosed and periodically re-verified by certified specialists, usually doctors or psychologists. There is a risk of excluding large numbers of students from higher education.

One accommodation is to allow more time to take tests and to allow the use of a word processor in cases where it is usually not allowed. A study showed that students who are allowed more time raise their scores an average of 100 points (out of a total of 1600) when they take the SAT. Overly competitive parents may seek that gain by claiming that their child has a disability.

"Learning-disabled students are much more likely to drop out of high school... and they graduate from college at much lower rates."

Learning Disabilities. (2003, April 4). *Issues & Controversies On File*. Facts On File News Services.

FROM SATAN TO NORMALIZATION

"People with intellectual disabilities have been consistently denied personhood; they have been seen as objects of pity, fear, or both; they have been oppressed; and, with the rise of the eugenics movement, they have been seen as a threat to the very quality of the human race."

Intellectual disabilities, unlike physical and sensory impairments (such as blindness and deafness), "strike at the very heart of classical and modern ideas of value and humanness."

In pre-scientific eras, a defect in the human mind was equated with being subhuman. Low intelligence was the sign of a person born to be a slave. Later, intellectual disability was a sign of possession by the devil. Early medical philosophers speculated about the origins of mental disorders. They looked at large ears, markings in the palm, and the shape and size of the head. Remedies were tried, including water treatment, bloodletting, ingestion of quinine, multivitamins, movement training, and faith healing.

In the *Age of Enlightenment*, we had the philosophical groundwork for the idea of personhood, and identity. Intelligence was key to the definition of personhood, differentiating people from animals. It was human to have rationality and consciousness, including self-consciousness. It was a quality that was God-given, and could not be attained through education. "Animals, idiots, and infants" were less than human. This was "an age that celebrated intelligence, beauty, perfection and rationality. The 'idiot' was dull, flawed, defaced with stigma and above all incurable."

In an *Abandonment Era* with the beginning of the industrial revolution, children with intellectual disability were abandoned to the countryside. There were many cases of feral children – those who survived exposure. This gave rise to the debate of nature versus nurture, and heredity versus environment – a sense that feral children could be recovered to society through education. A famous case of Victor, the Wild Boy of Aveyron ("l'enfant sauvage") drew the attention of leading physicians, who tried various methods to educate the boy.

One of the physicians was Edouard Seguin, who moved from France to North America, importing and refining methods of "idiot education." With medical colleges, he established the Association of Medical Officers of American Institutions for Idiots and Feeble Minded Persons, which eventually became the American Association on Mental Deficiency in 1933.

The earliest homes for foundlings, children born out of wedlock, were precursors of an *Institutionalization Era*. Catholic welfare societies took in foundlings and people with leprosy, mental illness, and intellectual disability. "Institutions exclusively for intellectual handicapped people grew out of the back wards of hospitals for people with mental illness."

The rising discipline of psychology contributed much to the view of intellectual disability. Alfred Binet founded psychometrics, the measurement of intelligence and the intelligence quotient (IQ). His first scale, published in 1905 at the Sorbonne, consisted of a series of life problems that required reasoning. His primary intention was to identify children who would benefit from special education, and he explored what that education would entail. Binet's intentions were later corrupted by the use of the IQ test to identify "morons."

A British scientist, Lionel Penrose, demonstrated that sterilization programs did not reduce the numbers of intellectually disabled people. His work influenced the cessation of the practice.

H.H. Goddard applied Binet's tests to identify children with difficulties. His scale included "idiots," "imbeciles," and "morons." The latter were trainable to function in society. He not only reduced the use of Binet's test to intelligence, he saw a link between low IQ and immorality – criminals, most alcoholics, prostitutes, and others on the fringe of society were innately defectives, or "morons." He linked immorality and stupidity. Thus he argued that society would save property and lives if it "colonized" or "put away" people in this category. By isolating them, society might "eliminate an enormous amount of crime, pauperism, and industrial inefficiency." A number of leading psychologists thus reinforced low expectations for cognitive development of those with low IQ scores, and reinforced a concept of racial superiority based on IQ. Later, we see whole races and ethnicities impugned as having "low IQ," justifying social subordination or rejection as immigrants.

Experience with training and education programs after the 1960s, and longitudinal studies, showed that people with various levels of intellectual impairment could live semi-independently. Their biggest disadvantage was not the impairment but the stigma of being labeled intellectually handicapped.

There many causes for the explosion of populations sequestered to institutions in the early part of the 20th Century. The eugenics movement claimed society needed to be protected from marginal people. The economic depression forced families to give up children because they could not care for them. Medical advances such as the invention of penicillin reduced mortality and prolonged the lives of inmates. State institutions were overwhelmed and became "hell holes" with minimal training and rehabilitation, and increasing neglect and abuse.

Behind the movement to take people out of the institutions and into the community was a new principle called *normalization.* The idea is to allow people with intellectual disabilities to learn appropriate normal behaviors and appearance (for their culture) and to minimize their differences or signs of deviance in order to gain social acceptance.

Normalization as an idea was developed by sociologists W. Wolfensberger and Ervin Goffman. Wolfensberger stressed that people with intellectual disabilities needed to be encouraged to adopt the appearance of conformity and to hide deviant characteristics, to reduce stigma. Goffman called this "passing." Later, Wolfensberger refined his idea, adding that "deviant" groups needed not just to conform and hide their deviance, but they needed to obtain valued roles in society.

Policy planners and service providers adopted this approach, as governments provided support for community-based care. Wolfensberger also developed standards and methods to evaluate services, as quality control. A weakness in the approach was the question of who determines what is "appropriate, normalized behavior" and "ordinary life."

The normalization principle represented a paradigm shift in the way services were provided to people with disabilities. It was consistent with the civil rights and independent living movements which emphasized personal choice and self-determination.

Some argue that deinstitutionalization was rapid in the 1980s because community services were no more expensive than institutional care, and the burden of funding shifted from the central government funding to states.

Scientific research flourished in this time period. Genetics, neuroscience, and biochemistry yielded new insights into the causes and types of brain dysfunctions, and also some treatments. We learned more about the development of the brain and effects on early learning.

One of the most significant advances was the development of early intervention programs. They offered an alternative to institutional care and provided parents with educational strategies to improve their child's capacity to function.

Parmenter, T.R. (2001). Intellectual disabilities- quo vadis? In G. Albrecht, K. Seelman & M. Bury (Eds.), *Handbook of Disability Studies* (pp. 267-296). Thousand Oaks, CA: Sage.

NUMBERS

In 1998, 3% of college students claimed to have learning disabilities.

School students diagnosed with Attention Deficit Disorder was in the range of 2%-9%.

By the Numbers: Learning Disabilities. (1998, February 6). Issues & Controversies. Facts On File News Services.

ADHD FACTS

ADHD was first diagnosed by Dr. George Still in 1902.

According to the Centers for Disease Control and Prevention, it affects 3 to 7 percent of school-aged children.

84% of parents in a survey gave their child prescription medicine. The medication helped more with behavior in school than with social relationships and self-esteem.

How to help a child with ADHD. *Consumer Reports*, October 2020, 8.

- ADHD is one of the most common neurobehavioral disorders of childhood
- It often lasts into adulthood
- Children with ADHD have trouble paying attention, controlling impulsive behaviors, and may be overly active.
- 3%-7% of school-aged children suffer from ADHD.
- Diagnosis of ADHD increased an average of 3% per year from 1997 to 2006.
- Boys are more likely than girls to have been diagnosed with ADHD.
- ADHD diagnosis is significantly higher among non-Hispanic, primarily English-speaking, and insured children.
- Prevalence varies substantially by state, from 5% to 11%
- 4% of children had both ADHD and Learning Disability
- The annual societal "cost of illness" for ADHD is estimated between $12,000 and $17,000 (2005 dollars)
- Workers with ADHD were more likely to have at least one sick day in the past month

ADHD Facts. Centers for Disease Control. Downloaded from www.cdc.gov/ncbddd/adhd/data.html on September 12, 2010.

AUTISM FACTS

- About 1% of children in the US have an Autism Spectrum Disorder (ASD)
- It is 4 to 5 times more likely to occur in boys than in girls
- It occurs in all racial, ethnic, and socioeconomic groups
- Studies in Asia, Europe and North America show a prevalence of 0.6% to over 1%
- About 13% of children have a developmental disability, including autism
- About 40% of children with an ASD do not talk at all
- 80% of parents saw problems in their child by 24 months
- Diagnosis of autism at age 2 can be reliable, valid, and stable
- Medical expenditures on average are $4,000 to $6,000 per year for AS

Autism Spectrum Disorder Facts. Centers for Disease Control. Downloaded from www.cdc.gov/ncbddd/autism/data.html on September 12, 2010.

INTELLECTUAL DISABILITIES

- A study of Atlanta shows 1.2% to 1.6% incidence of an intellectual disability (standard cognitive score of 70 or below).
- The cause of most intellectual disabilities is not known.
- Most common causes include genetic disorders such as Down syndrome, environmental factors such as prenatal alcohol exposure, infectious disease such as rubella, and metabolic disorders.
- .13% of babies born in the US each year have Down Syndrome

Intellectual disabilities among children. Centers for Disease Control. Downloaded from www.cdc.gov/ncbddd on September 12, 2010.

Universal Design (UD)

Modifications like curb cuts benefit many people, not just people with disabilities, for example, people pushing strollers, luggage, or loading carts, people riding bikes, older people, and those temporarily ill or distracted.

DEFINITION

Universal Design is a set of guidelines for designing everyday products so that they are more friendly and usable to a wider range of people, especially older people and persons with disabilities.

As persons with disabilities moved to live into public and community settings after the 1970s, everyone saw more instances where the way we build houses, public areas, computer interfaces, and appliances posed barriers that could be removed with conscious redesign. The disabilities rights movement heightened awareness of physical and interface barriers present in everyday environments. Experts in many countries started meeting to identify the range of barriers, examples, and standards, which resulted in publications by the International Standards Organization.

Everyone recognized that, internationally, our populations are changing. Life expectancy is increasing, which means more older people are active in our communities. More people survive injuries and illnesses and could function better if we designed differently. Consumers want greater convenience. Laws require accommodations including those facilitating physical mobility. Clearly universal design also benefits people who are carrying or moving children and objects, temporarily ill, or distracted. It is also consistent with the emergence of the field of ergonomics or human factors engineering --the applied science of designing equipment and workplace environments for greater productivity and health.

In the U.S., the Center for Universal Design at North Carolina State University acts as a research and education clearinghouse and provides technical assistance to people in the U.S. as well as foreign countries, developing plans and detailed descriptions of more accessible design.

The seven principles of UD are:

1. **Equitable use** – diverse abilities are considered
2. **Flexibility in use** -- diverse preferences are considered, for example reading versus hearing information
3. **Simple and intuitive use** – Easy to understand and not assuming a particular language, knowledge, or concentration level
4. **Perceptible information** – considers the context and environment, such as ambient conditions
5. **Tolerance for error** – accounts for accidental or unintended choices
6. **Low physical effort** – requires minimum strength and agility
7. **Size and space for approach and use** – considers wider variation in the size, posture and mobility of the user, for example, right or left-handed, people who need to stand, or to sit

EXAMPLES

Some examples of the application of universal design: curb cuts or sidewalk ramps, entrances without stairs, wide interior doors and hallways, lever handles on doors instead of knobs, buttons and controls that can be distinguished by touch, handles in bathrooms, auditory output from visual information displays (like maps), text labels on buttons and next to icons, ramps into swimming pools, closed captioning on television, and so on. The "good grip" kitchen utensils developed by OXO for arthritic hands proved to be an improvement that all consumers appreciated.

Universal Design is also called "Design for All."

The Center for Universal Design, North Carolina State University (2010). http://www.ncsu.edu/www/ncsu/design/sod5/cud/

UNIVERSAL DESIGN OF INSTRUCTION (UDI or UDL)

In the last two decades, Universal Design was applied to the design of instruction and learning experiences for students. It is called either **"Universal Design of Instruction"** or **"Universal Design for Learning."** It addresses the design of curriculum in terms of accessibility. UDI or UDL was described above in the section on higher education.

Assistive Technology (AT)

Fact sheets and case studies describe software or devices that available for many particular disabilities, such as autism, dyslexia, epilepsy, hearing impairment, learning difficulties, rheumatoid arthritis, vision impairment, and so on.

DEFINITION

Assistive technology is anything designed to improve the capabilities of persons with disabilities. It includes medical devices such as implantable pumps for diabetics, social devices that enable communication, and computer interfaces that give people access to information systems.

EXAMPLES

The array of devices and software available now defies the imagination of most people. New products are emerging nearly every day. Fortunately, there are groups whose mission is to monitor the market and suggest aids for different impairments.

- For low vision: large monitor, screen enlargement software
- For blindness: Braille printer, scanner and text scanning software, screen reading software
- For mobility impairments: voice-capture to computer, mouth stick for entry to computer, sip and puff switch, joystick, mouse that mounts on the head, alternative keyboards
- For learning disabilities: scanner and text scanning software, word processor with spell check and grammar check, software to help organize writing, speech output
- For hearing impairment: visual alternative to system sounds

University of Washington's DO-IT website has guides specifically for certain impairments, such as learning disabilities, sensory impairments, and mobility impairments.

It also has introductions to standards such as "Section 508" for computer systems designers, to make systems comply with regulations for accessibility.

There are videos demonstrating and explaining assistive technologies.

FACULTY ROOM

DO-IT has isolated resources that are particularly relevant for faculty.

For example, faculty with students having particular impairments can look up by:

- Low Vision
- Blindness
- Hearing Impairments
- Learning Disabilities
- Mobility Impairments
- Health Impairments
- Psychiatric Impairments
- Other Impairments

Each of these links offers links to case studies, associations explaining the disability, and typical tools and supports for this type of impairment. The case studies, for example, can include a narrative from a student with the impairment explaining what is helpful.

There are also resources around typical learning environments and experiences that often require accommodation:

- Large Lectures
- Groupwork
- Test Taking
- Field Work
- Science Labs
- Computer Labs
- Adaptive Technology
- Web Pages
- Distance Learning
- Artwork
- Writing Assignments
- International/Travel Programs

- Work-Base Learning

DO-IT, University of Washington (2010). Assistive technology used by DO-IT scholars. Downloaded on September 29, 2010 from http://www.washington.edu/doit/Brochures/Technology/tech.html

Also, The faculty room. Downloaded on September 29, 2010 from http://www.washington.edu/doit/Faculty/

COMPREHENSIVE HELP

Many educational institutions have already implemented student services, adapted facilities, and established policies for conforming to the law for reasonable accommodation. Promising practices, sample policies, case studies, legal considerations, information sheets, frequently asked questions, and tutorials are available in a knowledge center.

AccessIT links to many resources from the DO-IT project.

The National Center on Accessible Information Technology in Education, University of Washington (2010). AccessIT. Downloaded on September 29, 2010 from http://www.washington.edu/accessit/

PROFILE OF CATEA

The Center for Assistive Technology and Environmental Access (CATEA) at Georgia Tech is an example of comprehensive efforts to develop and support assistive technologies.

There are four laboratories:

1. Rehabilitation Engineering and Applied Research Laboratory (REAR)
2. Accessible Workplace Laboratory
3. Enabling Environments Laboratory (EE)
4. Accessible Education and Information Laboratory

Engineers, scientists, clinicians, and others are drawn from the Georgia Tech College of Architecture and other universities, the U.S. Veteran's Administration, and centers. They conduct research and teach courses, for example, in prosthetics and orthotics.

There are clusters of information organized for students, professionals in the field, consumers, and inventors. For example, students can find courses and employment information. Educators can find guides to assistive technologies and special techniques for teaching in general and teaching science, engineering and math subjects in particular.

Consumers can find information about thousands of assistive products. Inventors can contract for product testing services.

The Accessible Education and Information Laboratory provides information on education and technology, with a special focus on the accessibility of distance education for students with disabilities.

Current special projects are providing:

- information for university instructors who teach people with disabilities,
- guidance for high school teachers on making science, engineering, and math classrooms and labs accessible,
- a national public web site on assistive technology
- a network of older adults and people with disabilities to test prototypes, products and services designed for them
- Georgia Tech Research on Accessible Distance Education, tutorials and tools for creating accessible distance learning

Georgia Tech, Center for Assistive Technology and Environmental Access (CATEA) (2010). http://catea.gatech.edu/

INTERNATIONAL HELP

There are international resources as well, for example, Great Britain. Fact sheets from AbilityNet advise persons with particular disabilities as to what solutions—software or devices—are available. This list includes autism, dyslexia, epilepsy, hearing impairment, learning difficulties, rheumatoid arthritis, vision impairment and so on. For example, they explain special keyboards and voice recognition software.

AbilityNet. http://www.abilitynet.org.uk/index.php

PROSTHETICS: A RESPONSE TO THE DISABLED VETERAN

After World War II, public media and the arts sought to differentiate the image of the American worker in contrast with Europeans. The new "icons of American labor" were represented as fundamentally masculine, with qualities of "independence, reliability, efficiency, and resilience." The rise of industrial production during wartime was still fresh, and the blue-collar man was a hero and a symbol of corporate strength. The able-bodied man represented American vigor and promise.

At the same time, veterans were returning who were wounded, disfigured, or traumatized. There was concern about their re-integration, in the transition from wartime to civilian life and labor. The public media portrayed brave amputees who came back to get married, buy a house, get an education, and join the workforce. General Motors designed the Valiant car in 1945 to be operated by amputees. Patriotism, pride, and victory were themes linked to disability and masculinity. Disability (as represented by post-war amputees) was a symbol of sacrifice and patriotism.

An industry in the design and construction of prostheses flourished, addressing the anxieties of "the damaged male body" to a greater degree than with prior wars. New materials (acrylic, polyurethane, stainless steel) were found through materials science, and bioengineering developed as a field. Prosthetics refers to artificial additions, appendages, or extensions of the human body. The specialty came to be known as bio-cybernetics.

New artificial arms and legs represented a new body-machine interface for amputees and made it possible for them to look and act like "normal, able-bodied workingmen." "The association between amputees and state-of-the-art prosthetics research may have been an intentional strategy to link disabled veterans with the cutting edge of new scientific discoveries." For example, research produced acrylic eyes, dental prostheses, and acrylic facial parts (with racially consistent features). Later there were electronically controlled artificial limbs and cybernetic arms

Veterans and amputees did, however, suffer explicit discrimination from employers. The labor market was biased toward the physically fit and robust, in the rush to industrial productivity.

Public images of veterans sought to advertise progress in prosthetics research and assure the public that amputees suffered no loss of ability, personality, and manhood. Amputees were portrayed living "normal" and lives as self-confident, capable, masculine, and productive workers.

Ironically, the development of cybernetic arms led to the development of the industrial robot and robotic arms, that began to displace manual workers in large-scale manufacturing and industrial production by the mid-1960s. The purposes of rehabilitating amputees to turn them into productive laborers led to investment in the purposes of high production using robots on assembly lines.

Serlin, David (2006). The other arms race. In L.J. Davis (Ed.), *The Disability Studies reader* (2nd Ed.) (pp. 49-65). New York: Routledge.

CHANGING OUR PSYCHOLOGICAL RESPONSE

"We are obligated to shape a culture which uses the capacities of all our people, whatever their level." -R. L. Osgood

HIGHLIGHTS

- The entertainment media can, with intention, change and "undo" prejudice and stereotypes. This was demonstrated in the program Sesame Street for children, launched in 1969.
- Movies such as the biography of Dr. Temple Grandin in 2010 dispel the mystery and fear of impairments such as autism.
- There are learning experiences designed to raise unconscious emotional reactions and assumptions, and change them.
- Undergraduates can be educated in difference and diversity through a model called Intergroup Dialog, which is one course offering.
- There are many other "curriculums for tolerance," for children and adults, for example, from the Southern Poverty Law Center.
- We have learned much about unconscious bias and discrimination and how to reduce it, whether pertaining to gender, race, ethnicity, or disability. A number of approaches have worked, although they are not widely known or widely used: legal pressures to stop discrimination, social marketing, special education, representations in the entertainment media, and specially designed educational workshops.

INTRO

Can we re-educate ourselves and reduce or eliminate the psychological depth of stigmas associated with impairments? There are researchers who offer insights into unconscious bias, and education experts who specialize in teaching tolerance.

UNLEARNING STIGMAS

Is there a society with no stigmas? Some believe that the social integration of stigmatized groups – greater exposure to differences in a wide range of normal social activities -- reduces the onus of the stigma.

Learning stigmas is part of *early* social learning, and thus it can be very hard to unlearn stigmas abstractly, in a classroom. The economical, psychological, and social benefits of stigma to the dominant, powerful group sustain it. If you are in the dominant group, why forgo these benefits?

"From the perspective of cognitive psychology, **when people find it necessary or beneficial** to perceive the fundamental similarities they share with stigmatized people rather than the differences, we will see the beginnings of a real elimination of stigma." [italics mine]

"Stigmatized people have choices as to whether to accept their stigmatized condition … or continue to fight for more integration… Their cognitive and affective attitudes toward themselves as individuals and as a group are no small element in shaping societal responses to them. As long as they continue to focus on the negative, affective components of stigma, such as low self-esteem, it is not likely that their devalued status will change."

"People can choose to feel superior or inferior. … Each individual can choose to ignore social norms regarding stigma."

Social scientists have the challenge of better understanding the need to stigmatize -- the need for people to reject rather than accept others.

> Coleman, L. (2006). Stigma: An enigma demystified. In L.J. Davis (Ed.), *The Disability Studies reader* (2nd Ed.) (pp. 141-152). New York: Routledge. Originally published 1986.

EARLY AWARENESS OF DIFFERENCE IS NATURAL

A research lab found that children develop in-group preferences, specifically about race, before the age of one. Children naturally try to categorize everything, and they will identify with characteristics (such as skin color) most familiar to them. They will notice difference as early as six months. "It takes remarkably little for children to develop in-group preference." As they grow older, they decipher meaning associated with differences, with or without the help of adults. The study asked parents to discuss race with children 5 to 7 years old, in order to influence the assumptions the children made about race (e.g., who is "good" and who is "bad"). Very few parents actually managed to have the discussion. The rest, even though committed to the study, avoided the subject of race as too awkward and risky.

Bronson, P. & Merryman, A. (2009, September 14). See baby discriminate. Newsweek, 5.

THE POWER OF EDUCATIONAL TV: SESAME STREET AND OTHERS

The television show called Sesame Street was launched in 1969, aimed at preschool children. It transformed our assumptions about how much young children can learn, at preschool ages. After the show was introduced, many more children arrived in kindergarten knowing the alphabet and numbers. Sesame Street intentionally aimed to build cognitive skills, but it also intentionally programmed to build cultural awareness and tolerance. Characters of different races and characters with disabilities were included, showing tolerance and respectful interactions. Controversial topics like obesity and AIDS were raised. Although hard to prove specifically, it could be said that Sesame Street created generations of citizens with greater tolerance.

Guernsey, L. (2009, June 1). The show that counts. *Newsweek*, 54.

THE POWER OF ENTERTAINMENT MEDIA: TEMPLE GRANDIN

A recent movie educates the public about autism. It is a biography of Dr. Temple Grandin, who has autism. She did not speak, as a child, until three and a half years old. Her parents were advised to place her in an institution but declined. She became a scientist and a prolific author, currently working as a Professor of Animal Science at Colorado State University. She authored a best-selling book on autism called *The Way I See It: A Personal Look at Autism and Aspergers*. The movie "Temple Grandin" starring Claire Danes won two Emmy awards and contributed a startling personal account of autism that has educated both specialists and the public and dispelled many misconceptions about the condition.

Dr. Temple Grandin's Official Website.
http://www.templegrandin.com/ 2010.

CHANGING OUR OWN REACTIONS

It is possible to change our reactions to the differences posed by impairments we see in other people, and to change our emotional and intellectual response? Miller and Sammons have developed a method for exploring the kinds of feelings people have in response to disabilities. They offer exercises that lead people to reflect on unconscious and often negative dynamics, and make their feelings and thoughts both conscious and positive. The book suggests many "awareness activities" to draw out personal emotions and assumptions behind typical everyday reactions.

For example, "Find a place where you can observe a diverse group of people passing by, such as a shopping mall, an airport, or a train station. What appearance differences draw your attention? Which are familiar? … Do any appearance differences make you feel unsettled?" In other exercises, look for differences in movement. Then speech – different rates, vocabularies. Then behaviors.

Neuroscience offers insights into our reactions to things that are unfamiliar, unexpected, or unsettling. Our socialization exposes us to a certain range of types of people and behaviors that are typical or average. Socialization establishes and continually refreshes an emotional and cognitive comfort zone. We expect certain physical characteristics in other people, including the full array of body parts. We expect coordinated movement, speech rhythms and patterns, appropriate behaviors in social situations such as standing in lines and waiting, and a certain range of intelligence about our environment (using money, following directions, etc). Some extremes are more noticeable than others, for example, very tall or short people, shouting or muteness. The unconscious, primitive brain naturally detects differences, especially threatening differences. It automatically triggers heightened emotion in face of threatening or unsettling situations, for example, a scream, or unfamiliar sounds from a stranger. The rational brain can help us evaluate and override negative feelings when, in fact, differences are not a threat to us.

Among the differences we experience relative to disabilities that can confuse or frighten us:

- Difference in appearance – illness, anger, depression, missing body parts, disfigurement
- Difference in movement – use of wheelchairs, assistance dogs, canes, walkers
- Difference in communication – stuttering, slurring, tics, lip-reading and signing, use of a device to speak
- Difference in social behavior – lack of eye contact, standing too close or too distant, extremely fearful about arbitrary objects, inappropriately friendly
- Difference in learning – inability to understand signs or instructions, manage money, operate common appliances

The authors define a "4D Approach" to increasing awareness and changing personal reactions and interactions:

1. Detect: note the other person's disability and your internal reactions
2. Decide: decide what the nature of the difference is and your own options, choosing the ones that seem most useful
3. Do: behave in a new way
4. Debrief: reflect on your actions, what worked and didn't work, and what to try next time

People may have feelings of anger, curiosity, disgust, fear, interest, pity, shock, and so on. The method helps make the psychological process transparent and helps an individual treat the encounter as an opportunity for rational, self-conscious change.

For example, in encountering someone with a facial disfigurement, there are cultural premises that are evoked. We assume that physical beauty means happiness and success, and feel pity about the slightest irregularity.

In encountering someone with a problem moving, we assume that their thinking is impaired too. We associate standing and walking with independence, strength, and success. We prefer a fast pace of living as a sign of productivity and success. We must allow that people with having cerebral palsy, a stroke, Parkinson's, ALS, polio, multiple sclerosis and other diseases that limit their energy and mobility can still have active brains and personalities.

Similarly, regarding social behavior, we assume that people should not draw attention to themselves. Unusual behavior is "crazy" and probably dangerous. People are always responsible for their behavior. Yet people with mental disabilities can be unpredictable, out-of-control, confused, and socially inappropriate. Autism and mental retardation can cause unusual behaviors that are not controllable.

Regarding learning disabilities – we equate learning ability with independence. When we see someone is learning impaired, we assume they are doomed to dependency, which we consider a sign of weakness and failure. We are most comfortable with "average" intelligence and avoid the "too smart" as well as the "too dumb." We assume that intelligence is the ability to read and write, and don't imagine it is there without those particular skills.

The authors have a chapter on guiding children's reactions to disabilities in others, with exercises, and sample dialogs.

Everybody's Different is an excellent guide to emotional and social dynamics, and how to approach changing unconscious responses. It is practical, hopeful, and extremely useful to anyone who wants a personal exploration. The work could serve as a model for addressing our reactions to other types of "otherness" – gender, religion, ethnicity, race, age.

The book has chapters focused on particular disability types, such as different appearance, movement, communication, behavior, learning, and non-visible disabilities (mostly illnesses). At the end are suggested readings, films portraying characters with the type of disability, videos, and support and advocacy organizations.

> Miller, N. B. & Sammons, C.C. (1999). *Everybody's Different: Understanding and Changing Our Reactions to Disabilities.* Baltimore: Paul H. Brookes Pub. Co.

IMPLICIT BIAS TEST: RAISING THE UNCONSCIOUS

Can we tell if we are prejudiced? Project Implicit at Harvard University recognized that people are either unwilling to report their attitudes and beliefs, or, unable to report them because those attitudes and beliefs are unconscious. They designed an online test designed to uncover unconscious thinking and feeling. The test prompts for associations between words. It measures not so much the patterns of associations that the subject makes, but rather the time (in milliseconds) it takes to respond to a sequence of rapid prompts. Longer times suggest a difficulty making an association automatically. Among the Implicit Association test suite of experiments are tests of a subject's preference for young versus old people, preference for white versus black people, sexuality, gender and career, and gender and science. For example, it often reveals an association between "liberal arts" and "females" and between "science" and "males." There is an implicit bias test on association between "disabled" and "abled."

People taking the tests have been surprised at their implicit associations that indicate bias and discrimination. Some are dismayed at their scores because they have spent their careers and lives committed to fighting discrimination; their identity as a "fair" person is threatened. Subjects often want their results kept private because they consider them professionally damaging. The site warns: "If you are unprepared to encounter interpretations that you might find objectionable, please do not proceed further."

The Implicit Association tests are showing that that even the best *conscious* intentions and *conscious* reflection can cannot easily "undo" our *unconscious* schemas. The test can also measure change in attitudes and beliefs after a subject has learned to make different associations.

The implicit bias test is a good exercise to heighten your awareness of your own associations. The test can be conducted online, in private, by anyone.

Harvard University (2010). *Project Implicit.*
https://implicit.harvard.edu

INTERGROUP DIALOGUE MODEL

A method for educating with the goal of reducing prejudice based on identity and increasing tolerance has emerged in undergraduate education in the last 15 years. The approach called Intergroup Dialogue was initially developed at the University of Michigan and exported to many others.

Themes around social justice may focus on particular conflicts between social-cultural identity groups, for example gender, race & ethnicity, sexual orientation, white racial identity, religion, people with disabilities and people without disabilities.

Characteristics of the course are: small (12-16) face-to-face groups; members from two or more identity groups; trained facilitators; self-reflective and open conversation about differences; weekly meeting at least two hours for six to twelve weeks; basic readings outside of class. The process includes sharing perspectives from each identity group member, discussion of readings, reflection on socialization, delving into controversial issues, reflection on taking action and building alliances and sense of community.

"The participants explore commonalities and differences; examine the nature and impact of discrimination, power, and privilege; and find ways of working together toward greater inclusion, equality, and social justice." They question stereotypes, biases and misinformation.

The theoretical foundations of the model are in social psychology and intergroup contact theory on the conditions most effective for fostering relations between diverse groups, for example the use of active listening. It is founded in the concept of social justice and the value of understanding power and privilege in society. It incorporates theories from education, such as dialogic education and active learning. The model combines a traditional classroom approach whose goal is the transfer of knowledge, and approaches used in personal development that are more emotional and behavioral in focus.

The participants develop an awareness of themselves as members of a social identity group. They discover the impact of social identities (gender, race, disability, etc) on status in society. They learn how society values or devalues certain identity groups. By hearing from participants who are different from themselves, they gain an appreciation for structural inequality in society, and the possibility of participating in change.

Formal evaluations may use an assessment before and after the course, for example, measuring the change in participants' understanding (e.g., Structural Explanations for Inequalities Scale).

There is a growing infrastructure for the model, such as national training institutes, consultants and facilitators. The University of Massachusetts at Amherst applied the model for faculty and staff training. The University of Maryland engineering program required it for undergraduate students as leadership training.

Zuniga, Ximena, Nagdo, B.A., Chesler, M., & Cytron-Walker, A. (2007). *Intergroup dialogue in higher education: Meaningful learning about social justice.* NY: Jossey-Basse. J-B ASHE Higher Education Report Series (AEHE)

Zuniga, Ximena (1998). Fostering intergroup dialogue on campus: Essential ingredients. *Diversity Digest*. Downloaded July 31, 2010 from http://www.diversityweb.org/Digest/w98/fostering.html

CURRICULUM FOR TOLERANCE

Curriculum for K-12 classrooms is available from the website "Teaching Tolerance" maintained by the Southern Poverty Law Center since 1991. Their purpose is to facilitate education on tolerance, prejudice, discrimination, bias, and "difference" across all kinds of differences.

There are classroom activities for grades 3-6 and grades 6-8 on the Civil Rights Act and ADA, disability awareness, blindness, and learning disabilities, for example. There are professional development guides for teachers on dyslexia and ADHD, for example, as well as guides on how to teach about prejudice and discrimination generally and how to react to incidents in the school setting. There is a magazine called *Teaching Tolerance*, an e-newsletter, and reviews of books and videos that are additional resources for the classroom teacher.

Southern Poverty Law Center (2010). Teaching tolerance. http://www.tolerance.org/about

UNLEARNING BIAS & STEREOTYPES

An example of excellent materials for children that teach multicultural sensitivity and tolerance is a multimedia DVD called "Unlearning 'Indian' Stereotypes." It provides an introduction to Native American history. There are teaching ideas, lessons, photos and resources for classroom use. The DVD is among other materials focused on stereotypes and social justice.

The organization Rethinking Schools is like Teaching Tolerance in having a website of many resource materials with the mission of teaching tolerance.

> Rethinking Schools (2008). Unlearning 'Indian' stereotypes. DVD available from http://www.rethinkingschools.org . 12 minutes. Originally issued by the Council on Interracial Books for Children in 1977.

WHAT CAN I DO DIFFERENTLY?

- Recognize the historical and cultural forces behind negative reactions to disability and the dynamics that still linger unconsciously.

- See yourself in others, especially in persons with disabilities, and do unto others as you would have them do unto you: express respect, support, and friendship. Remember we are each one car accident, illness, or battle away from being a member of the group.

- See the Person, not the Disability. See the person as potentially yourself or someone near to you.

- Be aware of the kinds of accommodations that are mandated by law, and available. Make people aware of both assistive technologies that help persons with disabilities function in daily work life, and structural barriers that can be modified to remove barriers.

- Hire, promote, and support people with disabilities as equals.

- Make others aware of disability issues and rights in social and professional conversation.

- If you can, initiate or participate in programs that reach out to people with disabilities in school or in the workplace, as your personal advocacy.

- Work to acknowledge covert discrimination and bias, and to promote fairness in the workplace.

APPENDIX A: A LIST OF LAWS

HIGHLIGHTS

- Major legislation that provided for rehabilitation services followed large wars in the 20th Century, in response to the wish to reward soldiers for their service. The programs provided pensions, rehabilitation, and vocational training.

- In 1956, Congress introduced the **Social Security Disability Insurance**, to cover workers who acquired long-term disabilities.

- The **Supplemental Security Income** (SSI) was started in 1972 to cover individuals who had little or no work history. They receive modest benefits and automatically qualify for Medicaid. Increasingly, the applicants have psychiatric and addiction disorders.

- The **Vocational Rehabilitation Act of 1973** banned discrimination in programs associated with Federal funding. They required affirmative action in employment by Federal agencies. Section 504 provided for reasonable accommodation. Section 508 required that information systems be accessible.

- Two laws provide for a free and appropriate public education: The **Education for All Handicapped Children Act of 1975** and the **Individuals with Disabilities Education Act of 2004 (IDEA)**. They led to Federal support and regulation of special education.

- The **Americans With Disabilities Act of 1990 (ADA)** banned discrimination in employment, public accommodations, commercial facilities, transportation, and telecommunications. Public businesses and services must provide reasonable physical access and communication methods.

SUMMARY OF LAWS IN THE U.S.

Public policies in the form of laws express society's assumptions about the nature of disability and the right place in society for people with disabilities. They capture and reinforce our notions of social status, and our construction of what it means to be a person with disabilities.

The government, in effect, has defined who is disabled for certain purposes and what accommodations they need, especially in the past hundred years. Accordingly, our laws have defined needs for public services and subsidies. Public policies "… define who may work and who may receive public subsidies if they do not work; who may attend school and what services they will receive when they get to school; and whether people with disabilities have access to public transportation and private telecommunication systems."

An early turning point in U.S. policy on disability was a statement in 1907 asking for more assistance to disabled veterans, not because they were in need but because they should be rewarded for their military service.

"In every type of disability policy and program, from veterans' pensions to vocational rehabilitation, from social insurance to civil rights, notions of moral worth and social worthiness have played a central role in determining what individuals have qualified for benefits or protections." (p. 376, citation below) Social Security Disability Insurance (SSDI) is available to those who paid into the program via payroll taxes. The Supplemental Security Income (SSI) is mostly available to those who never worked, at a much lower level of benefits.

People with different impairments have gotten different levels of benefits. The different levels are not related to severity of impairment, but rather to the political mobilization of the group. For example, blind people have access to government contracts and to unique tax breaks.

Our government policies "reflect and reveal deep-seated cultural values about work, worthiness, dependency, and much more." (p. 376)

"The earliest national disability programs in the United States provided pensions for disabled military veterans." (p. 378) The pensions were justified in terms of moral obligation. They were broadened to include veterans of the Northern Civil War and thus became the first pensions for older citizens. Still, the justification was not impairment, but moral worthiness due to the soldier's sacrifice. The veterans' disability pensions anticipated Social Security.

The first European social insurance and pension programs, unlike American, offered entitlements to workers and to the indigent without the gloss of "deserving" or "undeserving." In America, the "morally undeserving," however needy, were not a national responsibility.

The first workers' compensation laws were modeled on the benefits for disabled military veterans – both medical and financial assistance was offered in return for service.

However, the laws placed the responsibility on states rather than the federal government. By 1921, 45 states had workers' compensation laws. There continues to be considerable variation across states.

The Smith-Sears Act of 1918 established vocational training for veterans. The Smith-Fess Act in 1920 extended vocational training and rehabilitation to almost all disabled Americans. By 1935 every state had one. The federal entity overseeing them became the Department of Health, Education, and Welfare. In 1940, "services were extended to people with disabilities who worked in sheltered workshops, to severely disabled people who were homebound, to individuals with disabilities in the paid workforce who required VR services to remain employed." (p. 382)

The rate of participation in SSDI increased rapidly through the late 1970s. The determination of eligibility was uncertain and subject to interpretation. Critics pointed to the program as a way out of work for some people with limited educational credentials or obsolete skills.

The SSI, started in 1972, provides case benefits to individuals with disabilities who have very low incomes, regardless of work history. The benefits are modest. Recipients automatically qualify for Medicaid. Recently, an increasing number of applicants have psychiatric and addiction disorders.

Vocational rehabilitation programs grew as part of President Lyndon Johnson's Great Society in the 1960s. There was popular support for public assistance after World War II. Advocates argued that the financial benefits of assisting persons with disabilities to enter the workforce exceed the costs of the services.

Expansion in the 1970s provided funding for local centers for independent living, known as CILs. This represented a shift to an emphasis on self-help, to viewing persons with disabilities as consumers, to a reliance on peer support rather than professional support, and to changing physical environments to enable independence. The objectives of vocational rehabilitation went beyond services to put people into paid employment, to broader services to enable independent living.

Gradually in the late 20th Century, the marginalization and isolation of persons with disabilities was reduced. With civil rights and anti-discrimination laws, the focus shifted from needs to rights. "Disability" was being redefined. Disability was not an inherent limitation of a person, but a limitation of the social and physical environment. Statutes in the 1930s already protected the rights of access to public places by blind people using white canes or service dogs. "These statutes were effectively the first American civil rights laws protecting people with disabilities." (p. 383)

In the 1980s, a presidentially appointed National Council on Disability proposed a bill that become the Americans with Disabilities Act of 1990 (ADA). It drew on Title V of the 1973 Rehabilitation Act and the Civil Rights Act of 1964, each of which defined discrimination regarding employment.

Assumptions about disability underlying public policies have shifted many times in the 20th Century. "Worker's compensation and SSDI assume that disability is incapacitating for paid employment. Vocational rehabilitation assumes that training and counseling can enable many individuals to overcome the functional consequences of their impairments and enter the workforce. Civil rights programs such as IDEA and the ADA assume that discriminatory environmental barriers create the marginal status of many Americans with disabilities." (p. 386)

The theme of who is worthy and "deserving" of benefits persists from earlier centuries. There is a fear that people who are able to work might get benefits. The claim to public support is also based on "innocence, the lack of personal responsibility for their condition, and suffering, or that their condition is particularly lamentable or pitiable. Embodying these characteristics may ultimately be far more important than the nature of one's actual impairment." (p. 388)

Many of the objections to the implementation of the ADA derive from a sense that claims are not justified. However, it is impossible to have a uniform definition that applies to everyone and all impairments, and all contexts. Government agencies must impose artificial uniformity in order to manage the range of conditions posed by individuals.

A number of public programs "have mandated the development of individualized service plans based on the needs of each service recipient," but still rely on boilerplate and templates to expedite the process. Precise definition is inadequate because of the range of impairments and circumstances, and it is also foiled by changes in either.

Ironically, the qualification of someone as "disabled" and deserving of services has the effect of making them a "special" person separate from others.

Scotch, Richard K. (2001). American disability policy in the 20th Century. In P.K. Longmore & L. Umansky (Eds.) *The new disability history: American perspectives* (pp. 375-392). New York: New York University Press.

LAWS

1918 — **Smith-Sears Veterans' Rehabilitation Act of 1918**
- States will establish and provide *vocational training for disabled veterans*, overseen by a federal board, with the purpose of rehabilitating veterans and facilitating their return to paid employment.

1920 — **Smith-Fess Act of 1920**
- The veterans training program under Smith-Sears is extended into a general federal-state *vocational rehabilitation program for almost all* disabled Americans. Clients had to have the potential for gainful employment. Services were limited to those with physical impairments, and over 16 years of age.

1943 — **Barden-La Follette Act of 1943**
- *People with mental disabilities* were made eligible for *vocational rehabilitation*.

1963 — **Maternal and Child Health and Mental Retardation Planning Amendments of 1963 (to the Social Security Act)**
- Establishes a new *mental retardation planning grant* program in the states- plans to improve residential, community, and preventive services

1963 — **Community Mental Health Centers Act of 1963**
- Establishes a network of *community support*

1968 ABA — **Architectural Barriers Act of 1968 (ABA)**
- All federally financed and constructed buildings must be accessible to persons with disabilities and elderly. New or newly altered buildings must meet ABA *architectural standards*.

1973 — **Vocational Rehabilitation Act of 1973**
- Programs conducted by Federal agencies or receiving Federal funding over $2500 (including contractors) *may not discriminate*

against persons with disabilities. Federal agencies must exercise *affirmative action in employment*.

- Section 504 provides for *reasonable accommodation*: access to programs, communication methods for people with hearing or vision disabilities, removal of physical barriers.

- Section 508 (added 1998) requires that electronic *information systems be accessible*, using software or hardware to provide outputs for visually impaired or hearing impaired people.

Regulations for the 1973 Act were released in 1977. They defined what constitutes discrimination on the basis of disability and explained requirements for the elimination of discrimination. Protests over the delay of regulations prompted the disability rights movement.

"The Rehabilitation Act of 1973 was pioneering … [it] laid the groundwork for many laws to come. It proposed a definition of disability that continues to be used. … Prohibits employment discrimination in the federal government and federally funded programs on the basis of either physical or mental disability. Section 504 of the Rehabilitation Act prohibits the same discrimination in the provision of public services."

Miller, N. B. & Sammons, C.C. (1999). *Everybody's Different: Understanding and Changing Our Reactions to Disabilities*. Baltimore: Paul H. Brookes Pub. Co.

1975	**Education for All Handicapped Children Act of 1975** (later IDEA)
	- All children with disabilities must receive a *free and appropriate public education*
	- School districts were required to locate children formerly excluded, provide diagnostic assessments, create individualized education plans (IEPs), provide adequate due process, and place children with disabilities in the least restrictive environment (LRE) for learning.

1984	**Voting Accessibility for the Elderly and Handicapped Act of 1984**
	• *Polling places* must be physically accessible. Voter registration must be available via telecommunications devices for deaf people (TDDs).
1986	**Air Carrier Access Act of 1986**
	• Persons with physical or mental impairments must have *access to public air transportation services*.
1988	**Fair Housing Amendments Act of 1988**
	• Prohibits discrimination in *housing* and related services.
1988 Tech Act	**Assistive Technology Act of 1988 (Tech Act)**
	• Provides formal, legal *definition of assistive technology*
1993 Motor Voter Act	**National Voter Registration Act of 1993 (Motor Voter Act)**
	• State-funded programs must provide forms, assistance, and transmittal services for *voting*.
1990 ADA	**Americans with Disabilities Act of 1990 (ADA)**
	• Persons with disabilities are protected from *discrimination* in employment, State and local government, public accommodations, commercial facilities, transportation, and telecommunications.
	• *Public transportation* services such as buses, subways, and trains must be *accessible*. Para-transit, or special services, can be used where structural modifications are not feasible.
	• *Public businesses and services* such as restaurants, stores, hotels, theaters, zoos, stadiums, etc., must provide *reasonable physical access and communication methods*. They must remove barriers where feasible.
	• Telephone and television carriers must provide for the use of *devices for deaf people* (telecommunications devices deaf people, or TDD). Television must provide for closed captioning.

- Persons with disabilities are defined as those with "a physical or mental impairment that substantially limits one or more major life activities."

- *Complaints* must be filed with the U.S. Equal Employment Opportunity Commission (EEOC).

On the 20th anniversary of the ADA, there are considerations for applying it in more areas. 911 call centers need to accept text or video messages from disabled people. Movie theaters could offer more movies with closed captioning. Office equipment and furniture could be more accessible.

O'Keefe, E. (2010, July 26). Americans With Disabilities Act marks 20 years. *Washington Post*.

The ADA made a big difference in opening employment opportunities for persons with disabilities. It is being amended and expanded. Initial fears about the cost of structural accommodation such as building ramps, widening doors, and the economic impact on small businesses diminished after there was experience with actual costs. Many disability-friendly features are now part of the design of new buildings.

1996	**Telecommunications Act of 1996**
	• Persons with disabilities should have access to *telecommunications services* using devices such as telephones, cell phones, pagers.
1997 CRIPA	**Civil Rights of Institutionalized Persons Act of 1997 (CRIPA)**
	• The U.S. Attorney General may investigate *conditions in prisons, detention centers, nursing homes, and psychiatric or mental institutions* to protect the constitutional right to healthy and safe treatment.
1998	**Assistive Technology Act of 1998 "AT Act"**
	• Repeals the Tech Act of 1988; *redefines assistive technology*
2004 IDEA	**Individuals with Disabilities Education Act of 2004 (IDEA)**
	Formerly the Education of the Handicapped Act of 1975 (P.L. 94-142)
	• Public schools must provide *a free education appropriate to*

individual needs. They must develop *Individualized Education Programs* (IEP's) for each child who is eligible. The IEP's must be developed by a team and reviewed annually. There is a due process for parents who disagree with a proposed IEP.
- Children may not be relegated to separate, custodial programs; the setting must be as close as possible to schooling provided to children without disabilities.

America is a leader among developed countries in laws, standards, and investment in the quality of life for persons with disabilities. Our level of accommodation is among the highest in the world.

APPENDIX B: TOP RECOMMENDED RESOURCES

Two community-maintained encyclopedias have short articles that provide quick explanations.

Wikipedia (English). http://en.wikipedia.org/wiki/Main_Page
> Search on, for example: disability, ADHD, autism, assistive technology, etc.

NationMaster. http://www.nationmaster.com
> World statistics and country comparisons on various topics contributed by anyone; an encyclopedia.

Key Websites

Center for an Accessible Society. http://www.accessiblesociety.org
> Disability issues information for journalists: a communications clearinghouse of credible information and quotable sources on national disability policy and independent living issues.

Society for Disability Studies. http://www.disstudies.org
> A scholarly organization that is dedicated to the cause of promoting the Disability Studies as an academic discipline. SDS seeks, through research, artistic production, teaching and activism, to augment understanding of disability in all cultures and historical periods, to promote greater awareness of the experiences of disabled people, and to advocate for social change. Publishes the *Disability Studies Quarterly,* which is published online.

National Organization on Disability. http://www.nod.org
> A private, non-profit focused on employment opportunities, conducting research on issues and trends, quality of life, and new employment practices.

ADAPT. http://www.adapt.org/
> A national grass-roots community that organizes disability rights activists.

Statistics	Rehabilitation Research and Training Center on Disability Statistics and Demographics (2010). *Annual disability statistics compendium 2010*. Downloaded from http://www.neweditions.net/statsrrtc/compendium2010.pdf
Participation in S&E	Seelman, K.D. (2001). Is disability a missing factor? In G. Albrecht, K. Seelman & M. Bury (Eds.), *Handbook of Disability Studies* (pp. 663-692). Thousand Oaks, CA: Sage. A discussion of modern technology development and the participation of persons with disabilities in the design of products. Argues that the industry would benefit from more than input and feedback from persons with disabilities as consumers. The industry is fragmented and serves small markets. It shows patterns of exclusion from the enterprise, and this is counter-productive.
Universal Design of Instruction	Scott, S., McGuire, J.M., & Embry, P. (2002). *Universal design for instruction fact sheet*. Storrs: University of Connecticut, Center on Postsecondary Education and Disability.
Universal Design of Instruction	Burgstahler, Sheryl (2009). *Universal Design of Instruction (UDI): Definition, principles, guidelines, and examples.* Downloaded from http://www.washington.edu/doit/Brochures/Academics/instruction.html on September 14, 2010.
UDI, Science, Math Assistive Technology	Georgia Tech, Center for Assistive Technology and Environmental Access (CATEA)(2011). SciTrain Project. http://catea.gatech.edu/scitrain The National Center on Accessible Information Technology in Education, University of Washington (2010). *AccessIT*. Downloaded on September 29, 2010 from http://www.washington.edu/accessit/
Special Education Categories	Texas Council for Developmental Disabilities, Project IDEAL. *Disability categories*. Downloaded from http://www.projectidealonline.org/overview.php on May 17, 2010
Special Education Categories	Price, Anne (2010). *Special education disability categories*. BellaOnline. Downloaded from http://bellaonline.com/articles/art35159.asp on May 25, 2010. Has good explanations for each category.

Laws & Public Policy	Scotch, Richard K. (2001). American disability policy in the 20th Century. In P.K. Longmore & L. Umansky (Eds.) *The new disability history: American perspectives* (pp. 375-392). New York: New York University Press.
History	Barnes, Colin (2010). A brief history of discrimination and disabled people. In L.J. Davis (Ed.), *The Disability Studies reader* (3rd Ed.) (pp. 20-32). New York: Routledge.
History	Braddock, D. & Parish, S. (2001). An institutional history of disability. In G. Albrecht, K. Seelman & M. Bury (Eds.), *Handbook of Disability Studies* (pp. 11-68). Thousand Oaks, CA: Sage.
History	State of Alaska, Governor's Council on Disabilities and Special Education (2010). *Disability history exhibit*. Downloaded November 2, 2010 from http://www.hss.state.ak.us/gcdse/history/
Disability Rights Movement	Johnson, R.A. (1999). Mobilizing the disabled. In Freeman, J. & Johnson, V. (Eds.). *Waves of protest: social movements since the sixties*. NY: Rowman & Littlefield.
Overview	Shakespeare, T. (2010). The social model of disability. In L.J. Davis (Ed.), *The Disability Studies reader* (3rd Ed.) (pp. 266-273). New York: Routledge.
History of Special Education	Osgood, R. L. (2008). *The history of special education: A struggle for equality in American public schools*. Westport, Conn: Praeger.
Experience of Disability	Murphy, Robert (1995). Encounters: The body silent in America. In B. Ingstad & S.R. Whyte (Eds.), *Disability and culture* (pp. 140-158). Berkeley: University of California Press. Originally published in 1987.
Stigma	Goffman, Erving (1963). *Stigma: Notes on the management of spoiled identity*. NY: Simon & Schuster.
Eugenics Movement	Davis, L.J. (2010). Constructing normalcy. In L.J. Davis (Ed.), *The Disability Studies reader* (3rd Ed.) (pp. 3-19). New York: Routledge.

Deaf Culture	Baynton, Douglas (2006). A silent exile on this earth. In L.J. Davis (Ed.), *The Disability Studies reader* (2nd Ed.) (pp. 33-48). New York: Routledge.
Bioethics	Asch, A. (2001). Disability, bioethics, and human rights. In G. Albrecht, K. Seelman & M. Bury (Eds.), *Handbook of Disability Studies* (pp. 297-326). Thousand Oaks, CA: Sage.
History of Psychiatry	Shorter, E. (1977). *A history of psychiatry: From the era of the asylum to the age of Prozac*. New York: John Wiley & Sons. Esp. Chap 1: The Birth of Psychiatry, pp. 1-32)
History of Psychiatry	Parmenter, T.R. (2001). Intellectual disabilities- quo vadis? In G. Albrecht, K. Seelman & M. Bury (Eds.), *Handbook of Disability Studies* (pp. 267-296). Thousand Oaks, CA: Sage.
ADHD	*ADHD Facts*. Centers for Disease Control. Downloaded from www.cdc.gov/ncbddd/adhd/data.html on September 12, 2010.
Autism	*Autism Spectrum Disorder Facts*. Centers for Disease Control. Downloaded from www.cdc.gov/ncbddd/autism/data.html on September 12, 2010.
Universal Design	The Center for Universal Design, North Carolina State University (2010). http://www.ncsu.edu/www/ncsu/design/sod5/cud/
Biographies	Disabled World (2006). Well known people with disabilities. Downloaded on August 3, 2010 from http://www.disabled-world.com/artman/publish/article_0060.shtml
Teaching Tolerance	Miller, N. B. & Sammons, C.C. (1999). *Everybody's Different: Understanding and Changing Our Reactions to Disabilities*. Baltimore: Paul H. Brookes.

APPENDIX C: ANNOTATED BIBLIOGRAPHY

OVERVIEWS (HISTORY AND GENERAL)

Pictoral	**State of Alaska, Governor's Council on Disabilities and Special Education (2010).** *Disability history exhibit*. Downloaded November 2, 2010 from http://www.hss.state.ak.us/gcdse/history/
	An excellent, colorful pictorial history and timeline, available as accessible HTML also. The best short introduction to history, with historical photographs as the main "narrative."
Quick Search	**Wikipedia (English).** http://en.wikipedia.org/wiki/Main_Page
	A community-maintained encyclopedia that has short articles with quick explanations. Search on, for example: disability, ADHD, autism, assistive technology, etc.
Statistics	**NationMaster.** http://www.nationmaster.com
	A community-maintained site on world statistics and country comparisons on various topics contributed by anyone; an encyclopedia. Includes topics related to disabilities.
Statistics	Rehabilitation Research and Training Center on Disability Statistics and Demographics (2010). *Annual disability statistics compendium 2010*. Downloaded from http://www.neweditions.net/statsrrtc/compendium2010.pdf
	An annual report that draws data from the U.S. Census Bureau's American Community Survey, 2009.
For Journalists	**Center for an Accessible Society.** http://www.accessiblesociety.org
	Disability issues information for journalists: a communications clearinghouse of credible information and quotable sources on national disability policy and independent living issues.
Academic	**Society for Disability Studies.** http://www.disstudies.org
	A scholarly organization that is dedicated to the cause of promoting the Disability Studies as an academic discipline. SDS seeks, through research,

	artistic production, teaching and activism, to augment understanding of disability in all cultures and historical periods, to promote greater awareness of the experiences of disabled people, and to advocate for social change. Publishes the *Disability Studies Quarterly*, which is published online.
Trends	**National Organization on Disability** http://www.nod.org
	A private, non-profit focused on employment opportunities, conducting research on issues and trends, quality of life, and new employment practices.
Advocacy	**ADAPT.** http://www.adapt.org/
	A national grass-roots community that organizes disability rights activists.
Advocacy	**American Association of People With Disabilities** http://www.aapd.org
	A cross-disability membership organization for advocacy. Founded in 1995 to unite the community. Issues annual statistics compendium.
Advocacy	**Disability Rights and Education Fund** http://www.dredf.org/
	Founded in 1979, is a leading national civil rights law and policy center directed by individuals with disabilities and parents who have children with disabilities.

HIGHER EDUCATION

Student Experience	**Beilke, J. R., & Yssel, N. (1999a). The chilly climate for students with disabilities in higher education. *College Student Journal*, 33(3), 364.**
	Higher education institutions have been willing to make physical accommodations for students with disabilities. Social acceptance on the part of faculty may lag, however. Researchers interviewed ten students with various visible and invisible impairments and documented their experience. The rise in this group is challenging the value system and culture of higher education.
Access, Universal Design for Instruction	**Scott, S., McGuire, J.M., & Shaw, S.F. (2003). Universal design for instruction: a new paradigm for adult instruction in postsecondary education. *Remedial and Special Education*, 24, 6 (November/December), 369-379.**

McGuire, J.M. & Scott, S.S. (2006). Universal design for instruction: extending the Universal Design paradigm to college instruction. *Journal of Postsecondary Education and Disability*, 19:2, 124-132.

Describes the origins of the principles of UDI, rationale, contexts for implementation, and examples of application in educational settings. The later paper describes three studies undertaken to confirm the validity of applying the UDI principles.

Science & Engineering, Access	**Georgia Tech, Center for Assistive Technology and Environmental Access (CATEA)(2011).** *SciTrain Project.* http://catea.gatech.edu/scitrain and http://www.catea.gatech.edu/scitrainU/login.php A research project looking at methods to train high school teachers of math, science, and computer science new methods that accommodate students with disabilities. The post-secondary section of the website offers a tutorial on accessible STEM teaching and what to do differently in large lecture classes
Universal Design for Instruction	**University of Connecticut, Center on Postsecondary Education and Disability (2010).** http://www.facultyware.uconn.edu Information on UDI principles and related information.
Universal Design for Instruction	**Association on Higher Education and Disability (2011).** http://www.ahead.org/ Advocates for disability services and promulgates standards for programs.
Universal Design for Instruction	**CAST (2011).** http://www.cast.org and http://www.udlcenter.org Runs the National Center on Universal Design for Learning, providing curriculum examples, technical assistance, courses, and information.
Assistive Technology Guides, Higher Education	**University of Washington, DO-IT (2010). Assistive technology used by DO-IT scholars.** Downloaded on September 29, 2010 from http://www.washington.edu/doit/Brochures/Technology/tech.html Also, **The faculty room.** Downloaded on September 29, 2010 from http://www.washington.edu/doit/Faculty/

Extensive resources on the availability and uses of assistive technologies in educational settings. Material customized for faculty. Testimonials on video by students. Guides to universal design for learning.

HISTORY

Disability Rights Movement

Johnson, R.A. (1999). Mobilizing the disabled. In J. Freeman & V. Johnson (Eds.), *Waves of protest: social movements since the sixties.* NY: Rowman & Littlefield.

An analytical social history of the disability rights movement, tracing the conditions that made it likely, related social movements, and pivotal events.

Disability Rights Movement

Shapiro, J. P. (1994). *No Pity: People with Disabilities Forging a New Civil Rights Movement* (1st ed.). New York: Times Books. Esp. Chapter 2, pp. 41-73: Shapiro, J.P. (1993). From charity to independent living.

A colorful, detailed story of the events comprising the early disability rights movement. For example, it tells the role of Ed Roberts, a post-polio quadriplegic at the University of California at Berkeley, who moved himself out of hospital settings and into independent living with others. The book has a very readable, journalistic style, with descriptions of key personalities and what they did.

Psychiatry

Lewis, B. (2010). A mad fight: Psychiatry and disability activism. In L.J. Davis (Ed.), *The Disability Studies reader* (3rd Ed.) (pp. 160-176). New York: Routledge.

The harsh treatment of people with mental illness provoked resistance, criticism, and rejection of the medical establishment. A person identified as mentally ill could lose individual rights, be confined to an asylum, and be subjected to treatments having dubious curative power. The Anti-Insane Asylum Society protested the use of confinement as a way of controlling, subordinating, and incarcerating people who were disagreeable. The Mad Pride movement in the 1970s brought together former patients who had had bad experiences. MindFreedom International evolved from Mad Pride and advocates for a revolution in mental health care: rights to choice in treatment, doctors, medication, place of care, and the right to care.

Group identity	**Davis, L.J. (2010). The end of identity politics: On disability as an unstable category. In L.J. Davis (Ed.), *The Disability Studies reader* (3rd Ed.) (pp. 301-315). New York: Routledge. Originally published in 2002.**

The category of "persons with disabilities" has evolved after it became a new political and cultural identity within the disability rights movement starting in the 1970s. People in the movement rejected the categorization of people with disabilities as medical problems in need of charity and treatment. They adopted the view that disability was socially constructed; it was not an inherent defect but a function of how society treated and helped individuals with impairments. With new laws, the category of who is a person with a disability has broadened to include people with back pain, for example, and obesity. Davis explores the question: "Is there a core identity there?"

Cultural myths	**Wendell, S. (2010). Toward a feminist theory of disability. In L.J. Davis (Ed.), *The Disability Studies reader* (3rd Ed.) (pp. 336-352). New York: Routledge. Originally published in 1989.**

There are many myths about the perfect body that contribute to the subordinate and negative treatment of persons with disabilities. One of our myths is that the body can be controlled, with proper medical care, and that disability is a failure. We prize independence and find dependence on the help of others humiliating. We avoid being confronted by, and fear, a body that suffers. We don't belief that people with disabilities can be productive workers. We (or our governments, society) regard the problem of an impairment as a family issue, and not a social responsibility. We spend more to keep people with disabilities out of sight rather than support their independent and productive lives.

Bioethics	**Asch, A. (2001). Disability, bioethics, and human rights. In G. Albrecht, K. Seelman & M. Bury (Eds.), *Handbook of Disability Studies* (pp. 297-326). Thousand Oaks, CA: Sage.**

A discussion of the biggest questions in bioethics from the point of view of the disability rights movement. For example, the right of newborns with impairments to be treated for conditions separate from their impairment, in order to prolong life. The use of prenatal testing and selective abortion to avoid giving birth to a child whose quality of life is deemed unacceptable. The right to sustain the life of someone with impairments that others deem intolerable. The right to die, or end life voluntarily, due to suffering, in spite of laws against suicide. In all of these situations, parents, family, and medical caretakers are subject to express discrimination and may act on assumptions based on misinformation. The disability rights movements' views are now articulated in, for example, "The Right to Live and To Be Different."

Intellectual Disabilities	**Parmenter, T.R. (2001). Intellectual disabilities- quo vadis? In G. Albrecht, K. Seelman & M. Bury (Eds.), *Handbook of Disability Studies* (pp. 267-296). Thousand Oaks, CA: Sage.**

A historical review of persons with intellectual disabilities. Some other general histories of disability do not specifically identify *intellectual impairments* as the most problematic for society. However, many of the worst treatments (infanticide, slavery, incarceration, sterilization, etc.) were aimed at this group. This history is more detailed, therefore, about what happened to "idiots" and the "feebleminded" over time. For example, testing for an intelligence quotient (IQ) became a defining measurement. Also, there is more detail about educational programs that were found to improve skills and behaviors, which enabled the integration of more people in this group into community and work.

Eugenics	**Davis, L.J. (2010). Constructing normalcy. In L.J. Davis (Ed.), The Disability Studies reader (3rd Ed.) (pp. 3-19). New York: Routledge. Originally published in 1995.**

A history of the rise of eugenics in the early 20th Century. Davis identifies some of the intellectual trends that led to eugenics, such as the idea of a "normal" body. For example, the foundation of statistics and the gathering of information about populations in the 19th Century led to notions that there was a standard population, and outliers. Eugenics took the idea of outliers further to deem them undesirable, drawing the conclusion that extremes (i.e., people with "defective" characteristics) should to be controlled and avoided, or eliminated from the population, to purify the human race.

Eugenics	**Hubbard, R. (2010). Abortion and disability: Who should and should not inhabit the world? In L.J. Davis (Ed.), *The Disability Studies reader* (3rd Ed.) (pp. 107-119). New York: Routledge. Originally published in 1990.**

A detailed account of the eugenics movement and its themes. It had a high period of influence in the U.S. from 1905 through 1935, leading to involuntary sterilization laws and the Immigration Restriction Act of 1924. IQ tests were used to identify "mental defectives." Many immigrants did not score well and there was a perception that there were whole ethnic groups that were inferior. Hubbard recounts the extent of sterilization programs in the U.S., and the use of abortion to prevent the birth of "defective" children.

Mental Illness	**Shorter, E. (1977). A history of psychiatry: From the era of the asylum to the age of Prozac. New York: John Wiley & Sons.**

A comprehensive history of the treatment of persons with mental illnesses and the emergence and evolution of psychiatry as a medical specialty. Covers the rise of asylums, trends in the philosophy and practice of treatment, the role of psychiatry within medicine and later in relationship to psychology and other non-medical treatment professionals. The movement away from Freud's psychotherapy to the reliance on drugs. Trends in the diagnosis of modern mental illness, including depression, Post Traumatic Stress Disorder, bipolar and schizophrenia.

Esp. Chap 1: The Birth of Psychiatry, pp. 1-32 and Chap 8: Frm Freud to Prozac (pp. 288-327) RC 438.S54 1977

Intellectual Disability	**Trent, J. (1995). *Inventing the feeble mind: A history of mental retardation in the United States*. Berkeley: University of California Press.**

Trent describes the history of care for persons with intellectual disabilities. He explores the themes of science (what are the causes and nature of the impairments), care (treatment and professional care-takers), and social control (society's fears and efforts to isolate this population). He covers the transition from institutionalization to community life and the trend toward "training centers."

History Prosthetics	**Serlin, David (2006). The other arms race. In L.J. Davis (Ed.), *The Disability Studies reader* (2nd Ed.) (pp. 49-65). New York: Routledge. Originally published 2004.**

A history of the development of prosthetics in the 20th Century. The impetus was to help wounded war veterans. Serlin describes some of the cultural and economic forces that shaped the modern industry. For example, new materials and the science of bioengineering made it possible to replicate the actions of arms and legs. However, the public portrayal of amputees still emphasized how "normal" and manly they were.

Comprehensive	**Barnes, Colin (2010). A brief history of discrimination and disabled people. In L.J. Davis (Ed.), *The Disability Studies reader* (3rd Ed.) (pp. 20-32). New York: Routledge.**

	A comprehensive history of the treatment of persons with disabilities covering all ages. Very rich detail, and identification of trends and themes.
Comprehensive	**Braddock, D. & Parish, S. (2001). An institutional history of disability. In G. Albrecht, K. Seelman & M. Bury (Eds.), *Handbook of Disability Studies* (pp. 11-68). Thousand Oaks, CA: Sage.**
	A good summary of the history of disability from ancient times to the present. Describes notions of impairment in Greece and Rome, beliefs about impairments during the Middle Ages and the rise of charity (e.g., hospices in monasteries), the fear of people with mental disabilities and control by putting them in institutions with criminals and poor people, and so on. Many roots of modern stereotypes, fears, traditions in treatment and response, and conditions of modern society can be found in our history.

SOCIOLOGY

Sociology	**Davis, Fred (1961). Deviance disavowal: The management of strained interaction by the visibly handicapped. *Social Problems*, 9, 121-132.**
	Normal people interacting with someone who is considered deviant have a strained interaction. People with a visible physical handicap suffer this social injury. There is a tendency for the normal to focus on the handicap. There are additional emotions evoked in reaction to the handicap. The full range of qualities of the handicapped person are in discord with the handicap. There is difficulty in assessing what activities are possible, due to lack of familiarity. The person with a handicap accepts the fiction that they are equal. Then, he emphasizes qualities that encourage the normal to identify with him, breaking through the focus on the handicap. Finally, he orients the normal about how to behave, making the interaction "normal," easy, and automatic.
Sociology	**Murphy, Robert F., Scheer, Jessica, Murphy, Yolanda, & Mack, Richard (1988). Physical disability and social liminality: A study in the rituals of adversity. *Social Science and Medicine*, 26(2), 235-242.**
	For many reasons, Goffman's idea that stigma explains the interactions between able-bodied people and people with disabilities is unsatisfying. A better model draws from the anthropological study of ritual, especially the concept of liminality. During rites of passage, initiates have a suspended social identity. They are isolated and separated from society in this state.

> The isolation of the physically handicapped is like the sequestering of initiates. They are in-between, socially, and deliberately excluded from society. Their state remains ambiguous and undefined. Other types of adversity (loss of income and status, catastrophic illness) evoke a liminal status also.

Inequality | **Baynton, D.C. (2001). Disability and the justification of inequality in American history. In P.K. Longmore & L. Umansky (Eds.) *The new disability history: American perspectives* (pp. 33-57). New York: New York University Press.**

Cultural assumptions about disability have been used to justify unequal and subordinate treatment of persons with disabilities. Groups are labeled deficient or defective (including women, categorically; immigrants) to justify limiting their participation in society, entitlement to rights, and control. Disability played a role in the justification for slavery: African Americans lacked sufficient intelligence to live independently and equally. If women were granted the vote they were incapable of acting responsibly. Both would get sick if they were subjected to education. Questioning unequal treatment has often involved questioning assumptions about inherent cognitive limitation.

Social Model | **Shakespeare, T. (2010). The social model of disability. In L.J. Davis (Ed.), *The Disability Studies reader* (3rd Ed.) (pp. 266-273). New York: Routledge.**

Explains the social model, which is the view that persons with disabilities have rights to inclusion, independence, and control over personal medical treatment. The view differentiates between an impairment, which is a physical limitation, and disability, which is a condition dependent on society's provision of assistance. Disability can be mitigated or removed. For example, many people with motor impairments can function independently and productively in society, given the right supports.

Stigma | **Brown, L.M.C. (2010). Stigma: An enigma demystified. In L.J. Davis (Ed.), *The Disability Studies reader* (3rd Ed.) (pp. 179-192). New York: Routledge. Originally published in 1896.**

An analysis of the roots of stigma, psychological and historical. This discussion is not presented as a theory so much as an explanation of the social-psychological phenomenon. It is also not focused on the stigma association with disabilities, but explore human reactions to differences of various kinds.

Stigma	**Goffman, Erving (1963).** *Stigma: Notes on the management of spoiled identity.* **NY: Simon & Schuster.**
	Goffman, Erving (2006). Selections from Stigma. In L.J. Davis (Ed.), *The Disability Studies reader* **(2nd Ed.) (pp. 131-140). New York: Routledge. Originally published in 1963.**
	A classic work in sociology offering a theory of social stigma. Goffman finds the historical roots for the idea of stigma in the Christian Middle Ages, when criminals were physically mutilated to identify them as morally bad. He says that stigma "spoils the social identity" of an individual. The book contains dozens of personal accounts from persons with disabilities.
Deafness	**Lane, H. (2010). Construction of deafness. In L.J. Davis (Ed.),** *The Disability Studies reader* **(3rd Ed.) (pp. 77-93). New York: Routledge. Originally published in 1995.**
	Lane describes the deep division among people who are deaf and their care-takers about whether it is better to learn to read lips or use hand gestures to communicate. The "oralists" hold that reading lips and learning to "pass" in society is a better strategy for integration and participation in society. The "manualists" maintain that sign language is a legitimate language, accelerates early learning, and recognizes the advantages of being proficient in a deaf community. Each side has a history, and implications for education, and support structures.
Deafness	**Baynton, Douglas (2006). A silent exile on this earth. In L.J. Davis (Ed.),** *The Disability Studies reader* **(2nd Ed.) (pp. 33-48). New York: Routledge. Originally published 1992.**
	A social history of the two competing camps regarding whether people who were deaf should communicate orally (learning to read lips and make sounds) versus manually (using sign language). He describes the consequences of the competition in establishing a controversy still unresolved. Each led to different institutional structures and identity issues for deaf people.
Cross-culture	**Whyte, S.R. & Ingstad, B. (1995). Disability and culture: An overview. In B. Ingstad & S.R. Whyte (Eds.),** *Disability and culture* **(pp. 3-34). Berkeley: University of California Press.**
	This is an introduction to a collection of papers that summarizes some of the cross-cultural themes in Disability Studies. It gives a perspective of

differences between Western approaches to disability versus others. Describes the emergence of anthropological work on disabilities.

Experience of Subjects	**Murphy, Robert F. (1987).** *The body silent*. NY: Henry Holt. **Murphy, Robert (1995). Encounters: The body silent in America.** In B. Ingstad & S.R. Whyte (Eds.), *Disability and culture* (pp. 140-158). Berkeley: University of California Press. Originally published in 1987. Murphy, an anthropologist, describes the experience of becoming a person with a disability, narrated from his professional view as a participant-observer. American values prefer the perfect young body and they contradict the realities of impairments. People recoil from imperfection and suffering in others. A person who becomes impaired suffers a social death and new identity and relationships.

EDUCATION AND ASSISTIVE TECHNOLOGY

Assistive Technology, Esp. Education	**Georgia Tech, Center for Assistive Technology and Environmental Access (CATEA) (2010).** http://catea.gatech.edu/ A center with four laboratories: for rehabilitation engineering, accessible workplace, enabling environments, and accessible education and information. One special project (SciTrain) is offering online courses to high school teachers on how to make their own science, math, and computer science instruction more accessible. It offers resources for teachers on specific accommodations for students with disabilities. There is also a database of references and publications for teachers.
Assistive Technology Guides	**The National Center on Accessible Information Technology in Education, University of Washington** (2010). AccessIT. Downloaded on September 29, 2010 from http://www.washington.edu/accessit/ A clearinghouse serving all educational institutions by providing information on assistive technologies.
Assistive Technology Guides	**AbilityNet.** http://www.abilitynet.org.uk/index.php A British charity helping disabled adults and children use computers and the internet by adapting and adjusting their technology. It has fact sheets by impairment (for example, dyslexia) or by type of hardware (e.g. keyboards). These make it easy to find products that will help an individual.
Special Education	**Lazerson, M. (1983). The origins of special education.** In J.G. Chambers & W.T. Hartman (Eds.), *Special Education Policies: Their history,*

implementation, and finance (pp. 15-47). Philadelphia: Temple University Press.

A history that highlights policy controversies in assigning students to special education, motivations for creating special education, and the impacts of legislation. Lazerson relates the emergence of special education to other trends such as the rise of immigration, fear of "defectives" and the eugenics movement, the evolution of public schools, legislation, and controversies about assigning children to special education.

Special Education	**Osgood, R. L. (2008).** *The history of special education: A struggle for equality in American public schools*. Westport, Conn: Praeger.

A comprehensive, detailed history of special education. Identifies major developments from the time of early public schools in the late 19th Century, including the treatment of children, the growing concern with controlling disruptive children in schools, and the emergence of special classes that worked to improve the behavior and skills of "challenged" children. New demands on special education come from increased numbers of students and the cost of highly customized educational attention.

Special Education	**Price, Anne (2010).** *Special education disability categories*. BellaOnline. **Downloaded from** http://bellaonline.com/articles/art35159.asp **on May 25, 2010.**

Has good explanations for each category of disability as it is used in special education.

Types, Special Education	**Texas Council for Developmental Disabilities, Project IDEAL.** *Disability categories*. **Downloaded from** http://www.projectidealonline.org/overview.php **on May 17, 2010**

A resource site for the implementation of The Individuals with Disabilities Education Improvement Act of 2004.

Special Education	**Watson, Goodwin (1938, March). "The exceptional child as a neglected resource."** *Childhood Education*.

A classic article that advanced the idea that children with disabilities were a neglected resource and should be developed. It argued for special education with a positive focus, rather than a deficit model (that the child needed to be fixed).

Learning	***ADHD Facts***. Centers for Disease Control. Downloaded from http://www.cdc.gov/ncbddd/adhd/data.html on September 12, 2010.

Statistics on prevalence, treatment, related issues, and economic cost.

Learning	***Autism Spectrum Disorder Facts***. Centers for Disease Control. Downloaded from http://www.cdc.gov/ncbddd/autism/data.html on September 12, 2010.

Statistics on prevalence, treatment, related issues, and economic cost.

Teaching Tolerance	**Zuniga, Ximena, Nagdo, B.A., Chesler, M., & Cytron-Walker, A. (2007*). Intergroup dialogue in higher education: Meaningful learning about social justice.* NY: Jossey-Basse. J-B ASHE Higher Education Report Series (AEHE)**

A model educational program for reducing prejudice based on identity. Developed at the University of Michigan and exported to many other undergraduate settings. Extensively evaluated for effectiveness, and refined over time. Students work in small face-to-face groups and challenge stereotypes, biases and misinformation.

Teaching Tolerance	**Southern Poverty Law Center (2010). Teaching tolerance.** http://www.tolerance.org/about

Offers curriculum for K-12 students and teachers on the subject of tolerance. Provides extensive resources on the subject.

Teaching Tolerance	**Harvard University (2010). *Project Implicit*.** https://implicit.harvard.edu

The primary website for Implicit Bias theory. Offers short online tests that any individual can take to test their level of bias in various associations (gender and science, disability, religion, race, sexual preference, etc.).

Teaching Tolerance	**Miller, N. B. & Sammons, C.C. (1999). *Everybody's Different: Understanding and Changing Our Reactions to Disabilities*. Baltimore: Paul H. Brookes Pub. Co. HV 1568 .M55 1991**

A guide to emotional and social dynamics at play in interactions with persons with disabilities. Offers practical exercises to uncover feelings and thoughts. Lists many resources. Authors are a psychologist and a therapist, so the emphasis is rare, and exclusively focused on response to impairments.

UNIVERSAL DESIGN

Clearing-house	**The Center for Universal Design, North Carolina State University (2010).** http://www.ncsu.edu/www/ncsu/design/sod5/cud/

A research and education clearinghouse that provides technical assistance and resources on Universal Design, developing plans and detailed descriptions of more accessible design.

Universal Design of Instruction	**Burgstahler, Sheryl (2009). Universal Design of Instruction (UDI): Definition, principles, guidelines, and examples.** Downloaded from http://www.washington.edu/doit/Brochures/Academics/instruction.html on September 14, 2010.

Resources on the Universal Design of Instruction.

Universal Design of Instruction	**CAST (2010).** http://www.cast.org/ and http://www.udlcenter.org/

Resources on the Universal Design of Instruction.

LAWS

Legal History	Scotch, Richard K. (2001). American disability policy in the 20th Century. In P.K. Longmore & L. Umansky (Eds.) *The new disability history: American perspectives* (pp. 375-392). New York: New York University Press.

A comprehensive review of laws that expressed society's assumptions about the nature of disability and the right place in society for people with disabilities. The government has defined who is disabled and what accommodations they need, what public services and subsidies they may receive, and who may work, attend public school, and have access to public facilities. The paper reveals cultural values about work, worthiness, and dependency, for example, through laws regarding veteran's benefits and vocational rehabilitation.

Summary	**U.S. Department of Justice, Civil Rights Division, Disability Rights Section (2005, updated 2006).** *A guide to disability rights laws: September 2005.* http://www.ada.gov/cguide.htm

A brief description of each law and its provisions, with links to further resources.

STATISTICS

Education — Aud, S., Hussar, W., Planty, M., Snyder, T., Bianco, K., Fox, M., Frohlich, L., Kemp, J., Drake, L. (2010). *The Condition of Education 2010* (NCES 2010-028). National Center for Education Statistics, Institute of Education Sciences, U.S. Department of Education. Washington, DC.

Has a section on statistics related to special education. Authoritative source.

National Population — Brault, Matthew (2008). *Americans with disabilities: 2005*. Current Population Reports, P70-117. Washington, DC: U.S. Census Bureau.

Authoritative statistics on demographics.

National Population — Brault, Matthew (2008). *Disability status and the characteristics or people in group quarters: a brief analysis of disability prevalence among the civilian non-institutionalized and total populations in the American Community Survey*. Washington, DC: U.S. Census Bureau.

Authoritative statistics on demographics.

GENERAL

Biographies — Disabled World (2006). Well known people with disabilities. Downloaded on August 3, 2010 from http://www.disabled-world.com/artman/publish/article_0060.shtml

Resources for the community, including biographies of role models and examples of famous people.

ACKNOWLEDGEMENTS

 This material is based upon work supported by the National Science Foundation, Research on Disabilities in Education, under Grant HRD 0622885. Any opinions, findings, and conclusions or recommendations expressed are those of the authors and do not necessarily reflect the views of the National Science Foundation.

Robert L. Todd, Senior Research Scientist at the Center for Assistive Technology and Environmental Access (CATEA) at the Georgia Institute of Technology directed the work. The host project "SciTrain" is developing online courses for high school teachers to instruct them in the creation of coursework for students with disabilities on subjects within science, technology, engineering, and mathematics.
http://www.catea.gatech.edu/

Dr. Ruta Sevo, an independent consultant, researched and wrote the report using the George Mason University library in Fairfax, Virginia. http://momox.org

The work was reviewed and benefited from valuable suggestions from:

- Dr. Steven E. Brown, Center on Disability Studies, University of Hawaii Manoa
- Dr. Phil Calkins, formerly with Equal Employment Opportunity Commission
- Dr. Margaretha Izzo, Nisonger Center of Excellence on Disabilities, Ohio State University
- Dr. Corinne Kirchner, Sociomedical Sciences, Mailman School of Public Health, Columbia University
- Dr. Jean K. Sando, Academic Affairs and Special Education, Minnesota State University Moorhead

Of significant help in the research were course syllabi for Disability Studies compiled by the Society for Disability Studies, which aims to broaden the field. It publishes the *Disability Studies Quarterly*.

One of its web pages offers a list of course syllabi contributed by scholars. Several syllabi in particular informed this paper. Thanks to:

> Phil Ferguson, Center for the Study of Disability, Education and Culture, Chapman University
>
> John Kramer, Institution for Community Inclusion, University of Massachusetts
> Manshaparven Mirza, University of Illinois at Chicago
> Terri Thrower, University of Illinois at Chicago
>
> Chris Lanterman, Center on Disabilities, Arizona State University
>
> Thomas J. Neuville, Department of Special Education, Millersville University
>
> Barbara Katz Rothman, Sociology, City University of New York

See http://www.disstudies.org/disability_studies_syllabi

www.ingramcontent.com/pod-product-compliance
Ingram Content Group UK Ltd.
Pitfield, Milton Keynes, MK11 3LW, UK
UKHW051256180426
11947UKWH00020B/1737